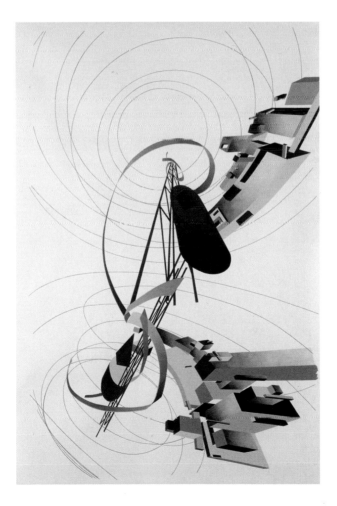

Philip Jodidio

ZAHA HADID

1950

The Explosion Reforming Space

TASCHEN

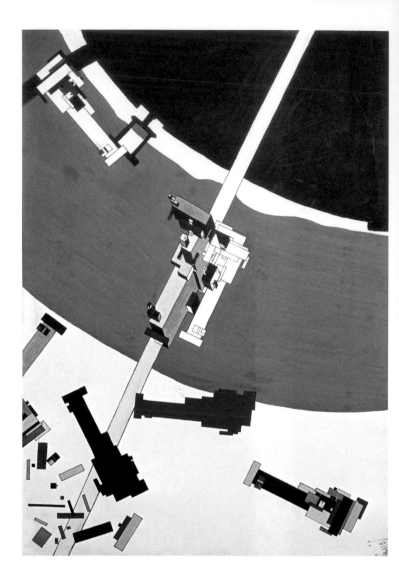

Illustration page 1:
*Tatlin Tower and Tektonik, "Worldwind", the Great
Utopia,* acrylic and watercolors on cartridge,
101.5 x 191 cm, 1992, Solomon R. Guggenheim
Museum

Illustration page 2:
Zaha Hadid, 2006, photograph by Jason Schmidt

Illustration page 4:
Horizontal Tektonik, Malevich's Tektonik, London,
acrylic on cartridge, 128 x 89 cm, 1976–77, San
Francisco Museum of Modern Art

© 2012 TASCHEN GmbH
Hohenzollernring 53, D–50672 Köln
www.taschen.com

Editor: Florian Kobler, Cologne
Design: Sense/Net, Andy Disl and
Birgit Eichwede, Cologne
Collaboration: Inga Hallsson, Cologne
Production: Tina Ciborowius, Cologne
Final Artwork: Tanja da Silva, Cologne

ISBN 978-3-8365-3072-9
Printed in Germany

To stay informed about upcoming TASCHEN
titles, please request our magazine at
www.taschen.com/magazine or write to
TASCHEN America, 6671 Sunset Boulevard,
Suite 1508, Los Angeles, CA 90028 USA;
contact-us@taschen.com; Fax: +1 (323) 463-4442.
We will be happy to send you a free copy of
our magazine which is filled with information
about all of our books.

Contents

The Explosion Reforming Space

Zaha Hadid, 2004
Photograph by Simone Cecchetti

Opposite page:
Vitra Fire Station,
Weil am Rhein, Germany, 1991–93
One of Hadid's first built works.

If not otherwise indicated, all quotes come from the interview with Zaha Hadid and Patrik Schumacher by the author, London, April 10, 2008.
1 "We might think of liquids in motion, structured by radiating waves, laminal flows, and spiraling eddies," says Patrik Schumacher.
2 Patrik Schumacher, "Zaha Hadid Architects – Experimentation Within a Long Wave of Innovation," in *Out There: Architecture Beyond Building*, Marsilio Editori, Venice, 2008, vol. 3, 91–92.

In a time of fluid uncertainty that envelops health and security, the economy, environment, and politics, it would seem natural that contemporary architecture should reflect a state of flux, and most probably take no discernable direction, wavering between ascetic minimalism, green proselytism, and neo-baroque decoration. Some, though, are courageous enough to make a wholehearted grasp at continuity, to dare say that there can be, indeed is, a new paradigm worthy of interest, even emulation. Few may be more qualified to issue this rallying call than Zaha Hadid, winner of the 2004 Pritzker Prize, and today the leader of a 300-strong office. It is Patrik Schumacher, Hadid's long-time collaborator, who signed a text in the 2008 catalog of the Venice Architecture Biennale that reads in part: "There is an unmistakable new style manifest within avant-garde architecture today. Its most striking characteristic is its complex and dynamic curve-linearity. Beyond this obvious surface feature one can identify a series of new concepts and methods that are so different from the repertoire of both traditional and modern architecture that one might speak of the emergence of a new paradigm for architecture. The shared concepts, formal repertoires, tectonic logics, and computational techniques that characterize this work are engendering the formation of a new hegemonic style: parametricism. Parametricism is the great new style after modernism. Postmodernism and Deconstructivism were transitional episodes that ushered in this new, long wave of research and innovation. Modernism was founded on the concept of space. Parametricism differentiates fields. Fields are full, as if filled with a fluid medium. From compositions of parts we proceed to dynamic fields of particles.[1] This sensibility has been both radicalized and refined over the course of 30 years of work. New modes of representation played a crucial part in making this possible."[2]

Whether the name "parametricism" sticks and, indeed, becomes that of a style or a recognized school of contemporary architecture or not remains to be seen, but it is clear that Zaha Hadid Architects has called attention to a method and an approach to architecture that has challenged many of its fundamental assumptions, beginning just over 30 years ago. Aside from her willingness to question geometry, or more precisely the very organization and spatial disposition of architecture, Hadid has shown a remarkable consistency and continuity in her thought over the entire period of her professional activity. Nor is this continuity tied to the kind of grid-driven style that animated Richard Meier or Tadao Ando, for example. Her built work and projects do resemble each other in terms of the fluidity of their plans and the movement of space and surface that she generates, but from the angular Vitra Fire Station (Weil am Rhein, Germany, 1991–93; page 28) to the more recent Dune Formations series of objects (David Gill Galleries, 2007), there is a spirit that casts doubt onto the architecture and furniture of the past. What if the many assumptions of architecture and design, from rectilinear form to the ways that buildings and furniture function, were all subject to question and, indeed, to profound renewal? If nature is capable of generating an endless variety of objects that have a fundamental legitimacy beyond any conceivable question, might architecture, the art of creating the built environment, not also be able to attain a similar legitimacy by reading context and function in new ways, by willfully creating voids as well as solids, by doubting the primacy of the right angle, itself very rare in nature? Would this be the artificial nature that many architects and thinkers have imagined?

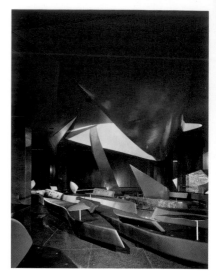

Moonsoon Restaurant, Sapporo, Japan, 1989–90
Conceived as a meeting of fire and ice.

Hybridize, Morph, De-Territorialize

Schumacher describes parametricism in formal terms that may seem less revolutionary than fundamentals of Hadid's architecture that clearly go beyond the formalist debate. "The program/style consists," says Schumacher, "of methodological rules: some tell us what paths of research to avoid (negative heuristics), and others what paths to pursue (positive heuristics). The defining heuristics of parametricism are fully reflected in the taboos and dogmas of our design culture. Negative heuristics: avoid familiar typologies, avoid platonic/hermetic objects, avoid clear-cut zones/territories, avoid repetition, avoid straight lines, avoid right angles, avoid corners ... Positive heuristics: hybridize, morph, de-territorialize, deform, iterate, use splines, nurbs, generative components, script rather than model."[3]

Just as Zaha Hadid has formed a remarkably coherent and consistent oeuvre over a period of 30 years, often returning to ideas first mooted early in her career, so, too, any description of her work may logically be made up of strands that, when brought together, describe her accomplishment not as a linear progression, but as an interwoven complex of idea, line, and form. It is thus by no means incongruous to leap back from the 2008 Venice Architecture Biennale and the manifesto "Experimentation Within a Long Wave of Innovation" to a moment 20 years ago, when Zaha Hadid first came to the attention of the general public.

The Oxford English Dictionary defines deconstruction as "a strategy of critical analysis ... directed toward exposing unquestioned metaphysical assumptions and internal contradictions in philosophical and literary language." Rendered popular by the French philosopher Jacques Derrida (1930–2004), deconstruction was used in the philosophical sense to explain some architecture. Derrida himself applied his thinking to architecture in a 1986 text about Bernard Tschumi's "Follies" in the Parc de la Villette in Paris, "Point de folie: Maintenant l'architecture." He spoke of "programmatic deconstruction," or a "general dislocation of the follies that seems to question everything that gave meaning to architecture until now. More precisely, that which related the order of architecture to meaning. The follies deconstruct, but not only, the semantics of architecture."[4]

The radical program implied in literary deconstruction was, indeed, not that far from the surprising forms that first emerged in public discourse with the 1988 exhibition curated by Philip Johnson and Mark Wigley at New York's Museum of Modern Art (MoMA), "Deconstructivist Architecture." Seven architects were selected for that

3 Ibid., 94–95.
4 Jacques Derrida, "Point de folie: Maintenant l'architecture," in *La Case Vide, La Villette, 1985,* Architectural Association, London, 1986.

**Landscape Formation One (LF One),
Weil am Rhein, Germany, 1996–99**
A seamless transition from landscape to
architecture.

show: Frank Gehry, Daniel Libeskind, Rem Koolhaas, Peter Eisenman, Zaha Hadid, Coop Himmelb(l)au, and Bernard Tschumi with his structures for the Parc de la Villette. The premise of the exhibition confirmed the idea of a radical about-face in contemporary architecture. "Architecture has always been a central cultural institution valued above all for its provision of stability and order. These qualities are seen to arise from the geometric purity of its formal composition," wrote Mark Wigley. "The projects in this exhibition," he went on to write, "mark a different sensibility, one in which the dream of pure form has been disturbed. Form has thus become contaminated. The dream has become a kind of nightmare."[5]

The Twisted Center of Modernist Purity

While the word "deconstruction" implied an act of destruction to many, Mark Wigley and the architects involved were pursuing a different agenda. "A deconstructive architect is not one who dismantles buildings, but one who locates the inherent dilemmas within buildings. The deconstructive architect puts the pure forms of the architectural tradition on the couch and identifies the symptoms of a repressed impurity. The impurity is drawn to the surface by a combination of gentle coaxing and violent torture: the form is interrogated," said Wigley.[6] Wigley and others related the work of the seven selected architects to the artistic revolution embraced by the Russian Constructivist and Suprematist movements shortly after the more political upheavals of 1917. "The Russian avant-garde posed a threat to tradition by breaking the classical rules of composition, in which the balanced, hierarchical relationship between forms creates a unified whole. Pure forms were now used to produced 'impure,' skewed geometric compositions."[7] It is a fact that drawings by Vladimir Krinskii reproduced in the exhibition catalog, or the Suprematist paintings of Kasimir Malevich, immediately bring to mind the work of Frank Gehry, or of the sole female participant, Zaha Hadid. It was Hadid's winning entry for the Hong Kong Peak International Competition (1982–83) that Johnson and Wigley chose to show at MoMA. Wigley wrote of this design for a health resort: "The club is stretched between the emptiness of the void and the density of the underground solids, domains normally excluded from modern architecture but found within it by pushing modernism to its limits, forcing it apart. In this way, the pleasure palace, the hedonist resort, is located in the twisted center of modernist purity."[8]

Twenty years later, Zaha Hadid and her partner Patrik Schumacher still refer to the MoMA exhibition. "The MoMA show concerned the contraction of two words," says Hadid, "deconstruction in the sense of thought and Constructivism, the Russian movement. Using those two words made it a hybrid thing. I believe that show was very important because it was the first time that people began to look at non-normative architecture. Unfortunately, in that period there was not great deconstructivist work done. None of us were building, which I think is a pity." Hadid's attachment to the work of the Suprematists was evident in such very early works as a meticulous painting executed for her thesis (*Horizontal Tektonik, Malevich's Tektonik, London*, acrylic on cartridge, 128 x 89 cm, 1976–77, San Francisco Museum of Modern Art). More than 10 years after her thesis, by the time of the MoMA exhibition, Hadid had gone on to apply the lessons of Suprematism to architecture in a way that took real structure into account. As an architect, and one formed in the circle of Koolhaas, she had had the intuition to realize that the time to change the art of building had come. Others involved in the MoMA exhibition, like Frank Gehry, left a strong mark on contemporary architec-

5 Mark Wigley, in *Deconstructivist Architecture*, The Museum of Modern Art, New York, 1988.
6 Ibid.
7 Ibid.
8 Ibid.

ture, but in Gehry's case it might seem that the art is all, a dancing symphony of forms that do, indeed, free buildings from their geometric constraints but may not address the deeper questions of the very logic of architecture to which Zaha Hadid has always been attached.

Breaking All the Rules but Drawing It Right

Although Wigley had affirmed that these architects were not engaged in dismantling, Patrik Schumacher has a slightly different take on the time: "You could see deconstructivism as a transitional style. It was a kind of creative destruction that set the scene for a positive agenda." Perhaps Wigley's own definition of the movement was too modest when it came to a figure like Zaha Hadid, who has gone on to redefine architecture in ways that defy the description of "skewed geometric compositions" employed in 1988. "The MoMA show was interesting," says Hadid today, "because it broke rules and went away from ideas of typology. The most critical thing was the breaking up of plan organization and section. Contrary to what some people thought, we were very precise. Our work was very precise in terms of geometry, it was not a cartoon. Breaking up typology, breaking the rules, these were very important steps because it was the first time that people became aware of these possibilities."

From the first, contrary to what some critics might have once suggested, Zaha Hadid's work was based not only on a full understanding of architecture but also of draftsmanship and of the profound relationships between the two. This fact of course immediately distanced her somewhat from the Russian revolutionaries of another era who were often engaged more in geometric speculations and aesthetic questioning than in any real desire to build. Hadid combined their challenge to accept spatial alignments with a real knowledge of architecture and that is what made her more than "deconstructivist." The combination of a cerebral revolution in architecture with the facts of construction and its possibilities has animated the work of Zaha Hadid Architects throughout the existence of the firm. When asked about her relationship to structural engineers, Zaha Hadid responds: "We always work with the same ones, although with different firms. We have established a system. That also allowed us to think of space in a different way and I think it has been a very exciting collaboration. Engineers don't come in at the end, they come in right from the beginning. They have to be involved in these enormous landscape structures that also hold the floor or support the roof." Rather than mistrusting engineers as any innovative architect might, Hadid has embraced their assistance, but in the process created a method that integrates their input into a completed whole. This process began even before she really built much, another proof of a constancy and drive that have today earned her a justifiable reputation as one of the most important creative architects in the world.

The Power of Innovation Revealed

Zaha Hadid was born in Baghdad in 1950 and studied at the Architectural Association (AA) in London, where she won the Diploma prize in 1977. She became a partner in the Office for Metropolitan Architecture (OMA) and taught with OMA founder Rem Koolhaas at the AA, where she led her own studio until 1987. She has held the Kenzo Tange Chair at the Harvard University Graduate School of Design; the Sullivan Chair at the University of Illinois, School of Architecture (Chicago); and guest professorships at the Hochschule für bildende Künste (Hamburg, Germany), and the University of Applied

Lois & Richard Rosenthal Center for Contemporary Art, Cincinnati, Ohio, USA, 1997–2003
The first American museum designed by a woman.

Bergisel Ski Jump, Innsbruck, Austria, 1999–2002
From the ski slopes to the Alpine sky.

Arts (Vienna, Austria), and was the Eero Saarinen Visiting Professor of Architectural Design at Yale University (New Haven, Connecticut, 2004). Few architects have had such a considerable impact through graphic works (paintings and drawings) and teaching as Hadid. Indeed, until a recent date, her built work might have been considered decidedly scarce by the standards of world-class architects. The first patron for one of her built works was Rolf Fehlbaum, chief executive officer of the furniture company Vitra. The Vitra Fire Station (page 28) entered magazines and books on contemporary architecture even before it was completed—its sharp, angular concrete design challenging the aesthetics of almost every known building. Fehlbaum was a member of the 2004 Pritzker Prize jury that gave its prestigious award to a woman for the first time with Hadid. "Without ever building," said Fehlbaum on that occasion, "Zaha Hadid would have radically expanded architecture's repertoire of spatial articulation. Now that the implementation in complex buildings is happening, the power of her innovation is fully revealed."[9]

The Vitra project was followed by Landscape Formation One (LF One, Weil am Rhein, Germany, 1996–99; page 32); the first museum built by a woman in the United States, the Lois & Richard Rosenthal Center for Contemporary Art (Cincinnati, Ohio, USA, 1997–2003; page 40); Hoenheim-Nord Terminus (Strasbourg, France, 1998–2001; page 36); and the Bergisel Ski Jump (Innsbruck, Austria, 1999–2002; page 38). Aside from a pavilion under the Millennium Dome in Greenwich, these were the completed works of Hadid when she won the Pritzker Prize. Lord Jacob Rothschild, Pritzker Jury Chairman, commented: "For the first time, a woman—and a very remarkable one—has been awarded the Pritzker Prize. Zaha Hadid, born in Iraq, has worked throughout her life in London—but such are the forces of conservatism that sadly one cannot find one single building of hers in the capital city where she has made her home. For more than a decade she was admired for her genius in envisioning spaces which lesser imaginations believed could not be built. For those who were prepared to take the risk from Vitra's Fire Station to a ski jump on a mountainside in Austria, to a

9 "Zaha Hadid Becomes the First Woman to Receive the Pritzker Architecture Prize," The Pritzker Architecture Prize, accessed on March 3, 2012, http://www.pritzkerprize.com/2004/announcement.

tram station in France, and more recently to a museum building in a town in the deep midwest of the United States, the impact has been transforming. At the same time as her theoretical and academic work, as a practicing architect she has been unswerving in her commitment to modernism. Always inventive, she's moved away from existing typology, from high tech, and has shifted the geometry of buildings. No project of hers is like the one before, but the defining characteristics remain consistent."[10]

Phaeno Science Center, Wolfsburg, Germany, 2000–05
Complex, dynamic, and fluid spaces form an artificial landscape.

Like a Chthonic Creature
At this defining stage in her career, when Hadid was 54 years old, quite young by the standards of world-renowned architects, she had just begun to leave her mark in the area of actual completed buildings, but one might ask if Lord Rothschild and others were right in putting the emphasis on her "unswerving commitment to modernism" or, indeed, in defining her work in terms of "shifted" geometry. In an essay about the LF One pavilion, the German architecture critic Michael Mönninger wrote: "The gardening pavilion rises from the ground like a chthonic creature whose direction of movement is linear through adaptation to the underground. The streamlined bends of the architectural path bundle are, if seen strictly, not space-creating but rather space-avoiding elements in between which the ancillary rooms, the café, the exhibition hall and the environmental center literally unfold in passing."[11] The words, 11 years earlier, of Mark Wigley immediately return with a new relevance: "... the emptiness of the void and the density of the underground solids, domains normally excluded from modern architecture but found within it by pushing modernism to its limits, forcing it apart." The Greek term employed by Mönninger, "a chthonic creature" (deities or spirits of the Underworld in ancient Greek mythology), might seem to be at the very opposite end of the spectrum when compared to a seminal work like Le Corbusier's Villa Savoye (Poissy, France, 1929), which sits on the ground so lightly, its pristine forms unrelated to anything so dark and unpredictable as the Underworld. Other architects like Peter Eisenman have experimented actively with forms related to the earth, such as plate

10 Ibid.
11 Michael Mönninger, in *LF One*, Birkhäuser Publishers, Basel, 1999.

Zaragoza Bridge Pavilion, Zaragoza, Spain, 2005–08
The gateway to Zaragoza Expo 2008.

tectonics, but, even as Zaha Hadid was winning the Pritzker Prize in 2004, it had long since become evident that, rather than an "unswerving commitment to modernism," she has embarked on a full-fledged questioning of that which is modern, of architecture itself. It may be that the comment of Bill Lacy, the Executive Director of the Pritzker Prize, was more to the point when he wrote: "Only rarely does an architect emerge with a philosophy and approach to the art form that influences the direction of the entire field. Such an architect is Zaha Hadid, who has patiently created and refined a vocabulary that sets new boundaries for the art of architecture."[12]

In fact, what the German critic identified as a relation to worlds beneath the surface in the LF One pavilion is quite literally a deep current in the work of Zaha Hadid. "This whole idea of the ground and ground manipulation starts from the very early projects," she explains. "I would say it goes back to the Residence for the Irish Prime Minister [Phoenix Park, Dublin, Ireland, 1979–80] because this project already involved the related idea of the artificial landscape, and also the studies for Vitra's extended fields, and then when we did the V&A [finalist competition entry for the Boilerhouse Gallery, Victoria and Albert Museum, London, UK, 1995], where this idea develops into an interior complex terracing as if a pastoral landscape began to be really sucked into the interior."[13]

The Dream of Pure Form Disturbed
Conceived as a winning competition entry just after the LF One pavilion was completed, the Phaeno Science Center (Wolfsburg, Germany, 2000–05; page 48) was described by the architect as a "covered artificial landscape" constituted of "craters, caverns, terraces, and plateaux." Its construction made use of individually fabricated formwork elements and special cast-in-place "self-compacting concrete" (SCC) that made its unusual shapes—some of them very sharp—possible. Though it does not sit as much in the earth as the LF One project, there is something of the great chthonic creature here too, only one that has fully emerged onto the surface. "The Phaeno is the most

12 "Zaha Hadid Becomes the First Woman to Receive the Pritzker Architecture Prize," The Pritzker Architecture Prize, accessed on March 3, 2012, http://www.pritzkerprize.com/2004/announcement.
13 Zaha Hadid interviewed in *El Croquis*, 103, Madrid, 2001.

ambitious and complete statement of our quest for complex, dynamic, and fluid spaces," said Zaha Hadid. "The visitor is faced with a degree of complexity and strangeness, ruled by a very specific system based on an unusual volumetric structural logic. The floors are neither piled above each other nor could they be seen as a single volume. The Phaeno's mass is supported and also structured by funnel-shaped cones protruding into it and extending from it. Through some of these funnels, the interior of the box is accessible: others are used to lighten the space inside, while some of them house necessary functions. This project combines formal and geometric complexity with structural audacity and material authenticity. A lot of time and energy was concentrated on achieving this result."[14] Mark Wigley's words—"the dream of pure form has been disturbed"—take on their full meaning here, though deconstruction itself seems far away. The concept of artificial nature is more to the point, creating an entity that might be imagined as a living creature, surely not formed like any animal of this earth, but put together with a driving logic that courses through its plan and section.

In describing two other projects, both for museums of contemporary art, conceived at about the same time, the Lois & Richard Rosenthal Center for Contemporary Art (page 40) and the MAXXI, the National Museum of XXI Century Arts (Rome, Italy, 1998–2010; page 66), Zaha Hadid unveils more of her process and thought and also suggests why her buildings pursue the same ideas but look so different. "What is ... similar between them is that both commissions are modernized sites which drew the insertion of a cultural program. In both cases, the urban context is expected to change in time and our respective projects are seen as agents of transformation ... The internal geometric complexity in the Rome project is a condensation of the different orientations of the surrounding contexts. One might say that the project discovers urban routes, which lie dormant within the neighboring context. Every shift in the field relates to a neighboring contextual condition. The Cincinnati project is equally contextual, although the way it is translated in each case feels very different. So the formal thing is not really decided in advance, it is just that these different formal systems emerge in

MAXXI, the National Museum of XXI Century Arts, Rome, Italy, 1998–2010
Walls intersect and separate to create interior and exterior spaces.

14 Zaha Hadid quoted in the press release, "Zaha Hadid Architects," November 23, 2005.

MAXXI, the National Museum of XXI Century Arts, Rome, Italy, 1998–2010
A 30 000-square-meter building designed for the Ministry of Culture and the Fondazione MAXXI.

the engagement with rather different conditions. One is much more imploded into the interior, the other has much more to do with perpetually negotiating between the interior and the exterior."

Looking for Natural Lines

A dense urban site or even a campus design like Hadid's proposal for the new campus center for IIT (Illinois Institute of Technology, Chicago, USA, 1998) are well suited to her complex patterns of interweaving lines and forms related to the location. However, in some instances, the site yields much less fundamental information. This is the case of her work in Dubai, for example the very large Signature Towers (Business Bay, Dubai, UAE, 2006–). What about context in an area that is literally rising from the sand? "In that case, you invent it," says Hadid. "The geometry of the context has an important impact. If you look at the IIT project in Chicago, there were lines that connected the project to certain schools. Views and vistas are not always important though. The Rome museum doesn't look like anything there, but it is influenced by the context. Every shift in that building relates to existing geometry." "Sometimes the project is so large that it creates its own context," adds Patrik Schumacher. "This is the case in Business Bay in Dubai, where the project exceeds half a million square meters. It is a highly integrated composition. It is one of the largest projects anywhere to have such a total coherence as a single integrated building." It would appear, then, that at a certain scale Hadid's projects become self-referential in terms of their coherence and internal logic, but the architect underlines that even where very large areas are concerned—such as in her Kartal-Pendik Master Plan (Istanbul, Turkey, 2006–), a scheme for an entire new city center in a former industrial area—fundamental connections are made to the place and to what might be called its natural energy. "If you look at a project like the master plan for Istanbul," she says, "each segment is very different, but it is recognizable as one place. We have looked for natural lines and addressed the water. We looked at the topography of Istanbul to create another topography on the other side."

Hadid's 70 000-square-meter Guangzhou Opera House (Guangzhou, China, 2003–10; page 76) offers other clues to her approach as viewed in the setting of a major Chinese city, currently in the throes of rapid expansion and modernization. Her "Conceptual Interpretation" of the site and the building combines references to geology ("twin boulders") and the layout of the city, including its riverfront: "Overlooking the Pearl River, the Guangzhou Opera House is at the heart of Guangzhou's cultural sites development. Adopting state-of-the-art technology in its design and construction, it will be a lasting monument to the new millennium, confirming Guangzhou as one of Asia's cultural centers. Its unique twin boulder design will enhance urban function by opening access to the riverside and dock areas and creating a new dialogue with the emerging new town." This description highlights a decided strength of Hadid's approach in that she makes reference to the reality of the city and at the same time to high technology, a source of pride in China, but in any case a link to the present and future. Her "Urban Strategy / Landscape" for the Guangzhou project makes it clear that the city itself and the new building is the landscape that she is forming and integrating: "The structure rises and falls at the foot of Zhujiang Boulevard, bringing together the two adjacent sites for the proposed museum and metropolitan activities. As an adjunct to the Haixinsha Tourist Park Island, the opera house presents a contoured profile to provide a large riverside focus to visitors. When viewed from the park at the center of the Zhujiang Boulevard, the opera house creates a visual prelude to the Tourist Park Island beyond. When viewed from the river, the towers of Zhujiang New Town provide a dramatic backdrop to the opera house and give a unified vision of civic and cultural buildings on a riverside setting."[15]

The key words in this description would appear to be "landforms" and "unified vision"—which in this instance clearly takes in not only the existing urban environment, but also a future museum near the site. As surprising as Zaha Hadid's forms may seem to some, they derive their legitimacy from their "seamless" integration into a site, or in the case of cities like Dubai, from an indisputable and continuous internal logic. Just as her furniture can be accumulated and disposed to define a continuous interior space, so her architecture may rise up out of the earth in its layered density, challenging assumptions about rectilinear "order" to create an artificial nature not unlike its real inspiration.

Waiting for FormZ

The paintings and drawings by Zaha Hadid for such earlier projects as The Peak have relevance not only for her celebrity, but also for the very nature of her design. Her creative process is one that she describes herself as being made up of layering and of multiple approaches to the same problem, accumulated and intertwined until a result emerges which has the legitimacy of a place and function. "It is important to emphasize that the line drawings have had an impact on the work," says Zaha Hadid. "There are things that resurface 10 or 20 years later. In the early years, I used a very layered system of sketching. All of the graphic techniques—layering in the drawing became layering in the project. The complexity in the drawing became complexity in the architecture." In this sense, it may be suggested that the early graphic work of Zaha Hadid may well have anticipated the computer revolution that has allowed her office to now design very complex structures. "I think the design method can be considered the precursor to computing," affirms Hadid. "The computer software called formZ, for exam-

15 Zaha Hadid Architects, "ZHA – Guangzhou Opera House – China – Conceptual Interpretation," January 24, 2008.

Guangzhou Opera House, Guangzhou, China, 2003–10
Linking the new city to the Pearl River and creating a "monument to the new millennium."

ple, is very similar to the drawing technique. The drawings remain more complex than computer drawings I think, though. Even when you have a kind of wild project, it is actually quite resolved and the drawings show that. The process has a kind of inherent logic to it. There was a correlation between the way the drawings were done and the architecture. The computer side led to research that made it possible to create complex buildings, but, fundamentally, the method has not changed. The system of doing it has changed but the ideas are still the same. If I look at some of my own sketches they look exactly like computer drawings. Now we know through a computer that you can actually do things that I sketch." Because she has already been involved in the highest levels of architecture for over 20 years, Zaha Hadid has worked astride the period in which computers have come to dominate design. Her own realization that her process and drawings closely resemble computer-assisted design might be a kind of self-fulfilling prophecy in which her own influence has helped to shape the very direction of software and the architecture it generates. More likely, because her creative process anticipated the computer, its emergence served only to vindicate and strengthen her resolve. While others were left trying to adapt Euclidean geometry and modernist form to the new world, Zaha Hadid began her quest in the realm of complex surfaces and multi-layered architecture.

Asked if she still sketches, Hadid responds: "Sometimes I do. I think that the reference is to one's own repertoire. You can reference back and there is a kind of knowledge. It is not so much about the power of the hand as it is the power of the idea. All

that work was not about how to do a nice sketch; it was really about how to develop an idea. After many takes and layers, the idea began to be developed, and it allows you to make these complex forms and to organize the interiors." Patrik Schumacher draws this line of reasoning further into the current work of the office when he says: "We are interested in nature as well, branching systems, rivers, and so on. We use these ideas to develop architectural space. Before, that was indicated through sketching and now it is done on a computer. The new tools have a great capacity to simulate environments and complex surfaces."

In the work of Zaha Hadid, there is surely a "reference to one's own repertoire," as she puts it, but there is also a radical, new approach to the relationship between architecture and nature, some of which has developed out of the increasing use of computer-assisted design. As Patrik Schumacher makes clear: "The nature reference is an old trope. It's not only the modernists; Renaissance and Classical architecture also reflected back and wanted to set its constructs within cosmology and an understanding of nature. In terms of the digital world, we see a proliferation of natural morphologies that are exciting and can be made to work and enrich the compositional and organizational repertoire—not just in terms of appearance, but also as organization patterns. For us [these morphologies] are navigation and orientation issues that can give more order to a complex environment."[16]

Inherently Lawful and Coherent
To the question of just how "natural morphologies" as manipulated through the use of the computer can improve architecture—a fundamental question where the work of Zaha Hadid is concerned—Patrik Schumacher responds: "The kinds of morphologies which come out of it are inherently lawful and coherent. There were prior attempts to establish this kind of coherency and law, either through talent and composing, where architects attempted to intuitively mimic the dynamic equilibrium, for instance, that you find in nature or to just restrict themselves to platonic geometries and symme-

Guangzhou Opera House, Guangzhou, China, 2003–10
The main 1800-seat auditorium designed with the latest acoustic technology.

16 Patrik Schumacher, interview, in MAD Dinner, by Ma Yansong, Actar, Barcelona, 2007.

Guangzhou Opera House, Guangzhou, China, 2003–10
Erosion, geology, and topography inform the architectural design.

tries—very basic orders. To have a more complex order, rather than some kind of ugly disorder, is possible with these new tools and, of course, there is a whole world of tools that exists for all sorts of purposes outside of architecture that can be harnessed, like RealFlow, etc. And their whole sensibility, in a sense, relates back to the perception of natural systems."[17]

It may indeed be that Zaha Hadid, whose extensive training in draftsmanship is evident in her careful drawings and paintings, does to some extent regret the days before computers took over. "I think that the work before analyzed and understood the context better than now. There was much more study and analysis of the site. Certain shifts were made because of site analysis. I don't think that there is any site analysis now. Context and site analysis are no longer part of the topic. There is no longer a discussion of context; they are mostly just objects that land there. The issue is not so much about computing or not computing. The problem with computing is that it isolates the object. It is inward-looking as opposed to outward-looking. It is an object. The nature of the piece is like that." Asked if she is today resigned to that reality, Zaha Hadid responds: "I am actually quite critical of it. We used to distinguish between the object and the field and I think it is because of technique that we don't anymore. There is no longer plan analysis." Patrik Schumacher for his part argues for what he calls "elegance" in contemporary architecture and specifically in the work of Zaha Hadid Architects. This elegance is found in an extensive search for a solution involving many studies and an incremental extrusion of the appropriate forms. "Each element is highly related to what is coming next and to its place within the overall scheme. That means that there is a lot of information embedded in these morphologies. It is a bit like a symphony. You cannot destroy a core of the melody, whereas in a cacophony you can take anything out and put it somewhere else. We now have the tools to do that in some of our projects. Everything means something, nothing is arbitrary." The cacophony Schumacher refers to is that which exists in a city such as Tokyo, a layered and embedded city if ever there was one, and yet not a system in which the "elegance" and new order sought by Zaha Hadid is at all apparent.

A Form of Natural Computing
It is here that Zaha Hadid's quest, expressed in a multitude of different objects, buildings, drawings, or even exhibition designs, reveals its ultimate continuity and the strong binding agent that holds together a career that is like no other in contemporary architecture. Though Hadid speaks of topography willingly, she does not often express her search in terms of the creation of an artificial nature. "We moved away from the idea of creating large objects and we looked at topography and the ground. We looked at the many layers of public space and how to interpret what is above ground and what is below. From there the natural move was to look at ... nature," says Hadid. Patrik Schumacher again makes the connection between the fundamental thinking of Hadid and its newly built forms. "There are millions of natural objects and each has its own coherency," he says. "It is open ended. If you have geological layers shifted against each other, there are always continuities. This is a form of natural computing if you want. The incident sits within a field of incidents where it makes sense. The way vegetation runs up a mountain makes sense. We are trying to bring this kind of logic into architecture. There is a sense of eloquent beauty and intuitive understanding that enters into the matter."

17 Ibid.

I Wouldn't Call It Sculpture

Zaha Hadid is unusual in that she creates furnishings or, more precisely, objects that are meant to form interior space. Recently, her work for David Gill Galleries and Established & Sons has taken on the sort of numbered and signed originality usually reserved for works of art, even if Zaha Hadid rejects the word "sculpture" to describe her pieces. She responds quite clearly to the question of how she came to design objects. "Of course we didn't really do architectural projects for a long time, and the question came up about how one could deal with furnishings in spaces that are not conventional. They also become part of the interior world, they become space dividers. When we did the Sawaya & Moroni things it was about having this kind of landscape or topography [Z-Scape Furniture, 2000]. The idea was to make a piece of furniture that is part of an ensemble which could be squished into a very small room like an environment, or you can spread it out." In fact, the discussion of what precisely links Hadid's object designs to her architecture is quite revealing in terms of the conception of both. "The transition between parts certainly applies to the design as well as the architecture," according to Patrik Schumacher. "The transition is smooth and not like bolting a tabletop onto four legs for example. It has to do with the spirit of the style—the total environment. In the hotel, we look at furniture as a space-making substance." The hotel referred to here is the Puerta América (Madrid, Spain, 2003–04) where Hadid created a seamlessly integrated floor and rooms made with thermoformed LG HI-MACS acrylics. In this astonishing environment, visitors are greeted by Hadid's edgeless surfaces as soon as they exit the elevator. Rooms have ceilings that become walls, desks that protrude directly from those walls, or even bathtubs that blend into their setting without any apparent edges. Practicality may be less important here than challenging the established order of right angles that has so long dominated design and architecture.

Mobile Art, Chanel Contemporary Art Container (various locations, 2007–11)
A series of continuous arches leads to a central courtyard.

The Diagonal Was the Beginning of All This

"I always think about how we can put the objects together," continues Zaha Hadid. "For the Seamless Collection [Established & Sons, 2006], I think of them as multiples so you can have a number of them, a tower of cabinets. They can always be seen as an isolated object or as many pieces together." The functionality described here, no matter how beautifully the objects flow together, is surely what makes Hadid react to the question of whether she would call this work sculptural. "No, I wouldn't use that word," she says bluntly. "Sculptural as opposed to what, flatware? Much mass-produced furniture was conceived as being flat. But the car—that was a whole idea about assembly that was never flat. For furniture now you can have pieces that are customized. You don't have to do flat shelves. These are definitely not minimalist—those are two worlds apart. It is about no 90° corners. The diagonal was the beginning of all this. The diagonal created the idea of the explosion reforming space. That was an important discovery."

The "explosion reforming space" that Zaha Hadid refers to here is amply visible in her drawings and paintings for The Peak in 1983. Where the straight lines and 90° angles of modernism had been the rule, in part for reasons of productivity, she actively pursued the diagonal, in her architecture as well as in her objects. Beyond the hard-edged tectonics of her earlier work on to the seamless smoothness of the Puerta América Hotel, the diagonal becomes a metaphor for the act of exploding space, of

Sheikh Zayed Bridge, Abu Dhabi, UAE, 1997–2010
Named for the founder of the UAE, the bridge has a total length of 842 meters.

questioning the most fundamental and "obvious" assumptions of architecture. A table has a flat top and four legs bolted on to it, a building is made up of an accumulation of Euclidian solids with hardly a worrisome void in sight. As complex as Zaha Hadid's work may sometimes seem, her real originality can be touched on in the questions she has asked about such obvious affirmations, the very framework of an architecture reproduced by rote for generations. Hers is, indeed, an explosion that reforms space.

When Hadid showed her Dune Formations (David Gill Galleries, 2007) at the Scuola dei Mercanti in Venice during the 2007 Biennale, she proved another most interesting point. Her burnt-orange aluminum and resin objects appeared to glide from one state or function to another within the confines of a very traditional Venetian building. Most of all, there was no inherent contradiction between the past and the future represented by the high-ceilinged rectilinearity of an old building and her flowing, curving shapes. Somewhat like natural objects that cannot be contested in their ultimate, formal legitimacy, so, too, the Dune Formations—inspired surely, as their name suggests, by the shifting sands of the desert—in no way seemed out of place in Venice. The viewer who senses this legitimacy may be coming close to understanding why Zaha Hadid is an important architect and designer. Her forms are like no other objects or buildings seen until now, notwithstanding any early connections to Russian Suprematism, for example, and yet their physical existence seems to be rooted in the earth as much as in computer-assisted design. Her layered complexity may not always achieve this kind of intuitive legitimacy, but when it does, as in the case of the Dune Formations, it opens new vistas for the future of art, architecture, and design.

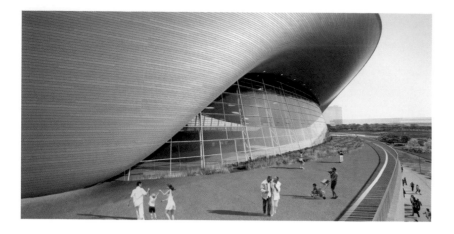

You Have to See It as Teamwork

An obvious transition has occurred in the career of Zaha Hadid, perhaps since she completed the Rosenthal Center in 2003. With 300 architects working under her orders, and projects underway from the UK to China, Zaha Hadid is very much in demand. She remarks candidly: "I think it is interesting to work that way, but I am taking advantage of the current situation. I don't think it could happen in one's lifetime many times, with the clients actually wanting this kind of work all over the world. I don't put any geographic limits on my work, but there are some countries where you have to be on the ground—it doesn't work with e-mails." Did the 2004 Pritzker Prize have anything to do with this explosion in demand for her designs? "I think so," she replies. "Of course we were doing things before, but the level of interest multiplied. Also, I think that people are interested in this kind of work. I have no idea if the same kind of thing happened to other Pritkzer architects at the same level as it happened to us." Asked how she deals with the quantity of new work, Hadid responds: "There is Patrik, of course, but we have lots of people who have been here for a long time. Many of the people were students of mine or of Patrik. We do things over many times to get them right. Our organizational structure is surely not a pyramid where I come up with an idea and hand things down. I think you have to see it as teamwork. Within the office we are involved in research that everybody understands."

The transition from a personal quest, whose first evidence might be the 1976–77 painting *Horizontal Tektonik, Malevich's Tektonik, London*, to the path of a globe-straddling architect has been managed by Zaha Hadid with an aplomb that obviously escapes many of her colleagues in the profession. Rem Koolhaas, who is six years older than Hadid, has also moved from a justifiable reputation as a theorist to running an office capable of building as astonishing a building as the CCTV Tower in Beijing, yet even OMA cannot boast the kind of project list that Zaha Hadid Architects is now engaged in.

The list of projects "on-site" published in this book, some of which will be finished by the time readers have the volume in hand, shows a remarkable geographic spread but also a continuous effort to redefine the very typology of buildings that will leave a mark, even for those who may question the style and dynamics of the Hadid office. With the MAXXI, the National Museum of XXI Century Arts in Rome, Hadid aims "to confront the material and conceptual dissonance evoked by art practice since the late 1960s," redefining not only the form but also the reactivity of museums to the art of

London Aquatics Centre, London, UK, 2005–11
Inspired by the fluid geometry of water in motion, the center seats 17 500 people.

Glasgow Riverside Museum, Glasgow, Scotland, UK, 2004–11
Like a wave flowing from the city to the waterfront.

today. Her Sheikh Zayed Bridge (Abu Dhabi, UAE, 1997–2010; page 72) weaves structural strands together, assuming a "sinusoidal waveform" over the channel between Abu Dhabi and the mainland, and questions and redefines the form of the bridge, usually the pure province of engineers, but surely a most "practical" object, here rendered dynamic enough to become "a destination in itself and potential catalyst in the future urban growth of Abu Dhabi." The London Aquatics Centre (London, UK, 2005–11; page 86) will be a noted element of the 2012 Olympic Games in the British capital, the first major structure in the city where Zaha Hadid has elected residence for so long. Its double-curvature parabolic roof and design, "inspired by the fluid geometry of water in motion," extend the range and nature of Hadid's references to nature, or perhaps more precisely to objects born of an artificial nature as legitimate as the sand dunes or flowing water she evokes. Further afield, the Heydar Aliyev Cultural Center (Baku, Azerbaijan, 2007–, under construction) makes a clear reference to topography, as the "building itself merges into the landscape ... blurring the boundary between the building and the ground." In the midst of designing so many large, complex buildings, Hadid has also taken the time to design a remarkable private house, the Capital Hill Residence (Moscow, Russia, 2006–12, estimated). With its lower volume partly embedded in a hillside in a "strategy that extends the exterior topography to the interior of the building," the house features a 22-meter-high tower that allows residents to look over the neighboring 20-meter-high trees.

Zaha Hadid is by no means the first architect to link her designs to nature. "The nature reference is an old trope," as Schumacher says. Significant figures, from Frank Lloyd Wright to Toyo Ito, have anchored their work in natural settings, but perhaps in a more literal way than Hadid. Did Fallingwater by Frank Lloyd Wright (Edgar J. Kaufmann House, Mill Run, Pennsylvania, USA, 1934–37) seem as futuristic to visitors in the late 1930s as the Capital Hill Residence will in the forest near Moscow? The seamless designs of Hadid, today given reality by cutting-edge technology and materials, never seem to descend into any mimicry of nature. The goal is elsewhere and that is why Hadid is no follower of Wright. This nature indeed rises up from the ground or the cityscape "like a chthonic creature" not born of any common experience, but somehow as unquestionable as an ancient myth. Geometry is here, but made up of the complex curves and overlaid patterns that sprang up from Zaha Hadid's mind only to be given form by the revolution in computer-assisted design and manufacturing that render the unique possible. The newness of modernism was pristine in its delicate avoidance of the world below in almost every sense. Architecturally speaking, modernist buildings only rarely venture in any visible way below grade. A basement is meant to be hidden, and above ground the reign of the sharply defined Euclidean solid is absolute. Elegant pilotis even kept the white virginity of the newly modern from being sullied by the earth. Ludwig Mies van der Rohe communed with a natural setting in a masterpiece such as his Farnsworth House (1945–50, Plano, Illinois, USA). For all its crystalline purity, the Farnsworth House was mocked at the time by the magazine *House Beautiful* as "a glass cage on stilts." With Hadid, nature may be artificial, but it is nature, with all its dark surprises intact.

An Architectural Language of Fluidity and Nature

Two recent ephemeral projects by Zaha Hadid serve to demonstrate the breadth of her interests and accomplishments, but also the voracity she displays in proving that her methods are applicable in the most diverse circumstances. Her Mobile Art, Chanel Contemporary Art Container (various locations, 2007–11; page 60) could hardly have a relation to a specific context since it was intended to move at the whim of the client, Karl Lagerfeld. Using sophisticated computer design, this exhibition pavilion employs what Hadid calls "an architectural language of fluidity and nature", or again, "an artificial landscape." Lagerfeld, an aesthete with an intuitive understanding of design, says of Hadid: "She is the first architect to find a way to part with the all-dominating post-Bauhaus aesthetic."

A second ephemeral work (*Lilas*, temporary installation, Serpentine Gallery, Kensington Gardens, London, UK, 2007) consisted in a series of three 5.5-meter-high parasols arrayed on a 310-square-meter platform. Clad in heat-welded PVC fabric, these parasols took their inspiration "from complex natural geometries such as flower petals and leaves," but above all seemed sculptural in their presence when they were erected on an extremely tight schedule for the Serpentine Gallery's Summer Party. The American sculptor Richard Serra has said that the difference between art and architecture is that architecture serves a purpose. The *Lilas* installation clearly served a purpose, but its presence and nature surely link it to the world of art, at least the art that remains connected to the world, to nature and to beauty. Nicolai Ouroussoff, the architecture critic of *The New York Times* has written of Hadid: "By collecting such disparate strands into one vision, she defiantly embraces a cosmopolitanism that is hard put to assert itself in our dark age. It is as close to a manifesto for the future as we have."[18]

Patrik Schumacher's theory of "elegance" with respect to the work of Zaha Hadid responds to the underlying question of just what the innovations brought forth by the firm mean, and how useful they are. "Why should we bother to strive for this increasingly difficult elegance? Does this elegance serve a purpose beyond itself?" he asks. And his response bears reading: "Contemporary architectural briefs are marked by a demand for evermore complex and simultaneous programmatic provisions to be organized within evermore complex urban contexts. Elegance allows for an increased programmatic complexity to coincide with a relative reduction of visual complication by means of integrating multiple elements into a coherent and continuous formal and spatial system. The general challenge is to find modes of composition that can articulate complex arrangements and relationships without losing legibility and the capacity to orient users. Elegance, as defined here, signifies this capacity to articulate complex

JS Bach Chamber Music Hall, Manchester, UK, 2009
Formed with a continuous ribbon of fabric for solo performances of the work of J. S. Bach.

18 Nicolai Ouroussoff, "Zaha Hadid: A Diva for the Digital Age," *The New York Times*, June 2, 2006.

Egyptian Pavilion, Shanghai World Expo, Shanghai, China, 2010
A single fabric ribbon continues from the façade into the exhibition space.

life processes in a way that can maintain overall comprehension, legibility, and continuous orientation within the composition."[19]

Where others ventured with gusto into the realm of the largely meaningless computer-generated "blob," Zaha Hadid emerged from the pre-computer era with ideas that the new technology rendered possible. Her precise, layered drawings were always meant to give rise to real buildings; she was never interested in pure aesthetics, even when she looked to the Suprematists for inspiration. It should be said that the Constructivists and Suprematists, unlike the Soviet-era masters of Russia's political destiny, really did imagine a brave new world. Hadid has broken not only the post-Bauhaus aesthetic, but more significantly the grid and the Euclidean solid. Her space ebbs and flows like the natural systems of branching evoked by Patrik Schumacher. Her work is at the juncture between architecture, art, and design, not always necessarily fully resolved because hers is an ongoing, formative process. "Avant-garde architecture produces manifestos: paradigmatic expositions of a new style's unique potential, not buildings that are balanced to function in all respects," says Schumacher with some bravado.[20] The adventure of Zaha Hadid is a remarkable one. Her success has been formed by a constancy and commitment to the belief that architecture and design need not be as they always were. Indeed, Bauhaus-inspired architecture did relate to industrial methods and the need for repetition to generate economies of scale. Hadid's concept of architecture, born of rigorous logic and design, yet freed of its Euclidean constraints, has been rendered possible by another industrial revolution driven by computer-assisted design and CNC milling. Desks can spring from walls and bridges can dance in sinusoidal undulations. Zaha Hadid has set architecture free, and it will never be the same again.

19 Patrik Schumacher, "Arguing for Elegance," *AD* (Architectural Design), London, January/February 2007.
20 Patrik Schumacher, "Zaha Hadid Architects – Experimentation Within a Long Wave of Innovation," *Out There: Architecture Beyond Building*, Marsilio Editori, Venice, 2008, vol. 3, 93–94.

1989–1990 ▸ **Moonsoon Restaurant**

Sapporo, Japan

Zaha Hadid created this restaurant in northern Japan after the 1988 MoMA exhibition "Deconstructivist Architecture" in which her Hong Kong Peak project was featured. Her client, Michihiro Kuzawa, also commissioned Aldo Rossi's iconic Palace Hotel in Hakata, southern Japan. Laid out on two floors of a nightclub—one for formal dining and the other for a "relaxed lounge"—the design features contrasting environments that the architect compares to fire and ice. The ground floor (ice) is conceived in tones of gray, using glass and metal. As the architect stated: "Tables are sharp fragments of ice: a raised floor level drifts like an iceberg across the space." Hadid refers to the celebrated local tradition of ice sculptures in winter in Sapporo as being a source of inspiration for this space. The upper floor, connected to the ground via a fiberglass spiral above the bar, was done in yellow, orange, and red. The spiraling connection bears early proof of Hadid's desire to create coherent environments, even when she indulges in specific, and rather exuberant, contrasts, as is the case in the Moonsoon Restaurant. Biomorphic sofas that can be configured in numerous ways are featured for the seating. Warmer and softer than the ground-floor design, the upper level contrasts not only in materials and colors but also in overall mood.

On the ground floor, the "ice" tones of gray and white dominate.

Opposite page:
Brilliant yellows and reds symbolizing fire meet cooler gray surfaces.

Right:
A plan shows the central sunken bar platform and a terrace to the left of the main area.

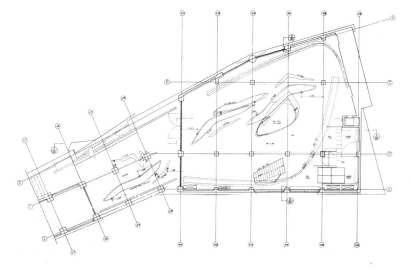

1991–1993 ▸ **Vitra Fire Station**

Weil am Rhein, Germany

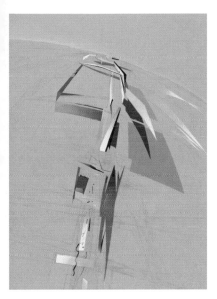

Prior to the Vitra project, Zaha Hadid was best known for her paintings and drawings.

Opposite page:
Hadid's first major completed building.

Right:
The splintered plan of the Vitra Fire Station.

Part of the campus of buildings by exceptional architects brought together by Vitra chief Rolf Fehlbaum, the Fire Station is one of Zaha Hadid's first efforts to translate her spectacular drawings into built form. Here, despite the surprisingly angular design, interior space is well managed to create an architecturally spectacular facility. Perhaps even more important, the architect has taken into account the large neighboring factory buildings and used the Fire Station to structure the street that it is set on. The building was "envisaged as a linear landscaped zone, almost as if it were the artificial extension of the linear patterns of the adjacent agricultural fields and vineyards," which also makes it an interesting predecessor to the nearby LF One project (page 32). Hadid meant the linear stretch of her building also to shield the Vitra complex from neighboring structures. According to the office description of the structure: "The space-defining and screening functions of the building were the point of departure for the development of the architectural concept: a linear, layered series of walls. The program of the Fire Station inhabits the spaces between these walls, which puncture, tilt, and break according to the functional requirements. The building is hermetic from a frontal reading, revealing the interiors only from a perpendicular viewpoint." It may be a moot point in this context that the structure was never really used as a fire station; rather it became the most visible and successful symbol of the architectural experimentation that Rolf Fehlbaum was willing to envisage, and the confirmation that Zaha Hadid's buildings would be as interesting as her drawings.

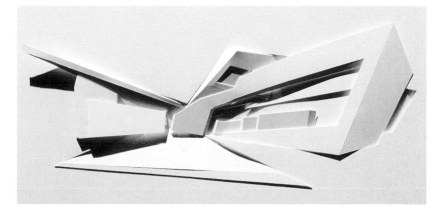

Interior spaces, also designed by the architect, confirm the spirit of the exterior.

Below:
Fire engines seem out of date in the striking building.

The raking angles of the structure might seem
more spectacular than purely functional.

1996–1999 ▸ Landscape Formation One (LF One)

Weil am Rhein, Germany

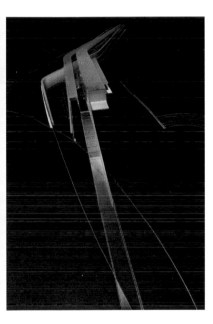

Zaha Hadid's drawing corresponds closely to the completed building seen left.

Opposite page:
Emerging from the pathways of the park, the architecture seems to emerge from its site.

Right:
At night, the low forms of the building have a dynamic, forward-leaning appearance.

Built for the 1999 Landesgartenschau (regional garden show) hosted by Weil am Rhein, this structure was conceived as a series of paths that in some respects integrate themselves directly into the surrounding gardens. Located close to the Vitra factories, where such architects as Frank Gehry, Tadao Ando, Álvaro Siza, and Zaha Hadid herself have built, this 750-square-meter building includes a restaurant, offices, and an exhibition space. Made of three distinct concrete strands, the concrete structure is inserted into its environment so as to maximize its temperature stability both in winter and in summer. With its terraces and walkways, the building seems not to be an alien presence as its complex design might suggest, and as Zaha Hadid's reputation might have led some to expect. Rather, it blends gently into the landscape and fulfills its assigned role admirably well. The fact that this design has its source of inspiration in the natural environment is clearly confirmed by Hadid, who says: "This exhibition hall for an international gardening show is part of a sequence of projects that try to elicit new fluid spatialities from the study of natural landscape formations such as river deltas, mountain ranges, forests, deserts, canyons, ice flows, and oceans. The most important general characteristics of landscape spaces, as distinct from traditional urban and architectural spaces, are the multitude of subtle territorial definitions as well as the smoothness of transitions ... This means that we abandon architecture and surrender to nature; rather, the point here is to seek out potentially productive analogies to inspire the invention of new artificial landforms, pertinent to our contemporary complex and multiple life processes."

1998–2000 ▸ **Mind Zone Millennium Dome**

London, UK

Walls, and floors, are part of a continuous surface that forms exhibition space.

Opposite page:
The Mind Zone was one of 14 Millennium Dome exhibitions.

Right:
The completed structure had a surface of 2500 square meters.

Situated beneath the Millennium Dome, Zaha Hadid's Mind Zone stood out with its spectacular cantilevered steel structure. As the designer says: "Our minds are amazingly complex machines and our aim is to unravel some of their mysteries in a truly memorable fashion." Working with a number of talented artists, such as Ron Mueck, Gavin Turk, Langlands & Bell, Helen Chadwick, and Richard Deacon, Hadid succeeded in creating spaces that appear to defy gravity and to prepare the visitor for the technologically oriented exhibits within the pavilion. Clearly, there was some danger for Hadid in participating in this circus-like assembly of pavilions, but she showed by the force of her design that good architecture can impose itself even in difficult conditions. One of 14 individual exhibition spaces within the Millennium Dome, the Mind Zone was controlled by Hadid both from an architectural and a curatorial point of view, with the assistance for the artist liaison of Doris Lockhart-Saatchi. Here, as in many of her works, she formed a continuous surface "that allows for a fluid journey through the space," encompassing floors, walls, and ceilings. According to the architect's description of the project: "As a narrative strategy, the three elements complement the primary mental functions—'input,' 'process,' and 'output'—represented variously through perspective and visual distortion, explanatory exhibits, sculpture, computers, audiovisual installations, and interactive elements. The design strategy avoids being overtly pedagogical and is interactive and thought provoking." Essentially made of synthetic materials such as lightweight transparent panels with glass-fiber skins and an aluminum honeycomb structure, the pavilion, destined to last one year, sought to "create an ephemeral temporal quality."

1998–2001 ▸ Hoenheim-Nord Terminus and Car Park

Strasbourg, France

An architect's sketch shows the lines of force that mark the project.

Opposite page:
With its skewed columns and thin concrete roof, the building provides shelter in an otherwise open space.

Below:
An aerial view shows the effort made to connect the parking area to the architecture.

As part of a tramway system installed by the eastern French city of Strasbourg, one of the two homes of the European Parliament, Zaha Hadid created a station and car park for 700 vehicles at the northern end of Line B (Hoenheim Gare to Lingolsheim, a distance of 14.7 kilometers). It may be interesting to note that the city had invited such reputed artists as Mario Merz and Barbara Kruger to participate in the first phase of the tramway operation, and that Hadid's interventions, in many images, almost appear to be more of a work of art on a large scale than a piece of architecture. As the former mayor of Strasbourg and former French Minister of Culture Catherine Trautmann put it: "Public transport is an especially effective means of increasing people's awareness of the art of their time and an outlet for contemporary art distinct from traditional venues." Hadid imagined the design as a set of overlapping fields or directional lines that are formed by the movement of cars, trams, bicycles, or people on foot. Made up of a waiting space, bicycle storage area, toilets, and a shop, the station is animated by lines that continue in the overall pattern of the plan, appearing inside sometimes as narrow openings in the concrete ceilings or walls. The parking spots, each marked by thin vertical lamps, are initially organized along a north–south axis, but then curve gently in a rhythm suggested by the boundaries of the site. Like the LF One (page 32) or Vitra (page 28) projects, the Strasbourg project experiments with the idea of "artificial nature ... one that blurs the boundaries between natural and artificial environments" with the goal of "improving civic life for Strasbourg," according to the architect.

1999–2002 ▸ **Bergisel Ski Jump**

Innsbruck, Austria

Created in 1926, the Bergisel Ski Jump has been well known almost since its construction, and was the site of the 1964 and 1976 Winter Olympic competitions. The schedule of international ski jumping events is such that local authorities could allow only one year from demolition to opening the new facility. Cleverly, the Ski Jump includes a steel-plate-clad café situated 10 meters above the jumping ramp, and it is apparent in the design that the Austrian Ski Federation wanted to create a monument as much as they sought a high-quality sports facility. Seating 150 people, the café boasts a 360° view of the city and mountain scenery. In spite of local resistance to contemporary architecture of notable quality, both Hadid and Dominique Perrault (Innsbruck Town Hall) have succeeded in breaking into this Tyrolean stronghold of traditionalism. Forty-eight meters tall and seven by seven meters on the ground, the concrete structure has already permitted long flights, such as the 134.5-meter jump achieved here by Sven Hannawald in January 2002. Hadid has described the structure as an "organic hybrid"—a sort of mixture of a tower and a bridge—but it succeeds in abstracting the speed of motion and flight that characterizes the most spectacular of winter sports events.

Because it is surrounded by the forest, the building has an iconic, isolated presence.

Opposite page:
Night lighting and dramatic forms contribute to the exciting presence of the ski jump.

Right:
A drawing shows how the tower links to and, in a sense, emerges from the slope.

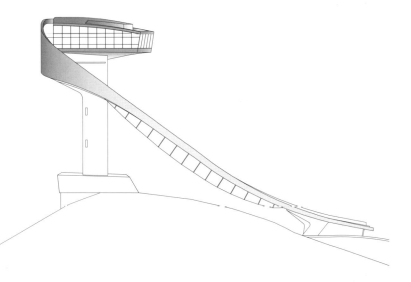

1997–2003 ▸ Lois & Richard Rosenthal Center for Contemporary Art

Cincinnati, Ohio, USA

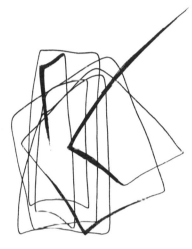

A sketch by the architect sums up its design and location in surprisingly simple form.

Opposite page:
Densely occupying its corner site, the building seems to be based on geometric stacking.

Right:
A bird's eye view of the structure shows its massing.

With the opening of the Rosenthal Center, Zaha Hadid became, surprisingly enough, the first woman to design an American art museum. Even more surprising for the usually angular and complicated Hadid, her new museum fits nicely into a city street of mixed architectural merit. Indeed, the only thing that signals the presence of an architectural "star" in this unlikely location is the closed succession of cantilevered boxes that looks onto 6th Street. True, Marcel Breuer's Whitney Museum on Madison Avenue presents similarly blind volumes of stone to the street. Then, too, this is the very institution that dared to defy the strictures of puritan America by exhibiting the controversial photographs of Robert Mapplethorpe, becoming embroiled in a famous obscenity trial. Measuring about 8500 square meters, this is not a very large building, but it does signal the arrival of Hadid as a serious builder as opposed to a largely theoretical designer. Poured-in-place concrete floors seem to curve effortlessly into walls near the entrance, and visitors see heavy painted black steel ramp-stairs that rise almost 30 meters up to skylights. Each flight of stairs weighs 15 tons, as much as the construction cranes could carry. This staircase is the central mediating feature of the center, leading to the exhibition space and providing a continuous focal point for the movement of visitors. Hadid's architecture relies on the art it will exhibit to bring its exhibition spaces to life, even if some artists may find her spaces challenging or difficult. This is less an act of artistic freedom than Gehry's Guggenheim Bilbao, but it remains a significant step forward for quality architecture in the context of America's often barren provincial cities.

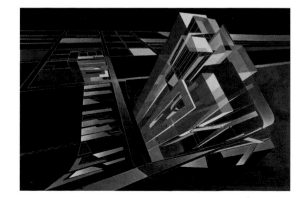

Sharp angles and vertiginous space.

Below left:
The forms of Hadid's buildings resemble her drawings and paintings.

Below right:
In the building, a work by Iñigo Manglano-Ovalle, *Cloud Prototype No. 1*, 2003.

Opposite page:
Hadid's dramatic slicing of the building.

2001–2005 ▸ **Ordrupgaard Museum Extension**

Copenhagen, Denmark

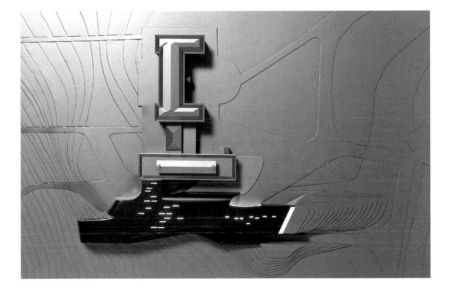

A model shows the new building (right).

Opposite page:
The basic form of the building is a folded concrete shell with a broadly glazed front.

Below:
The surface of the extension reflects the surrounding forest.

For this extension of the existing Ordrupgaard Museum, a Danish state museum for 19th-century French and Danish art lodged in the former mansion of the collector Wilhelm Hansen, Zaha Hadid again called on the idea of a distinct relationship between the landscape setting and the new building: "The new extension seeks to establish a new landscape within the territory of its architecture, at the same time allowing new relations with the existing conditions. The logic of the existing landscape is abstracted in the geometry; new contours extend into the collection developing an alternate ground where occupancy and use are extended." Built by the Danish Ministry of Culture, Fonden Realdania, and Augustin Fonden, the new structure is 87 meters long and 20 meters wide, plus a five-meter passage to the old structure. Made of cast black lava concrete, the structure's complex curving geometry suggested an on-site molding process with the self-consolidating concrete pressed into forms from below or pumped into an outer shell through holes. With walls curving into ceilings or floors, the Extension experiments successfully with continuous space, where the straight lines that characterize the original museum are the exception rather than the rule. Indeed, the architect insists on fluidity even in the transition from inside to outside and from one building to the other. "The critique of the edge is thus replaced by a notion of fluid interaction between the garden and the interior program," she says, "and it acts as a constant instrument of gradation that allows for different conditions to appear without necessarily breaking the volume up." Glazing shows the relationship of the building to its topography, while openings in the continuous shell provide ample opportunities for movement from one area to another.

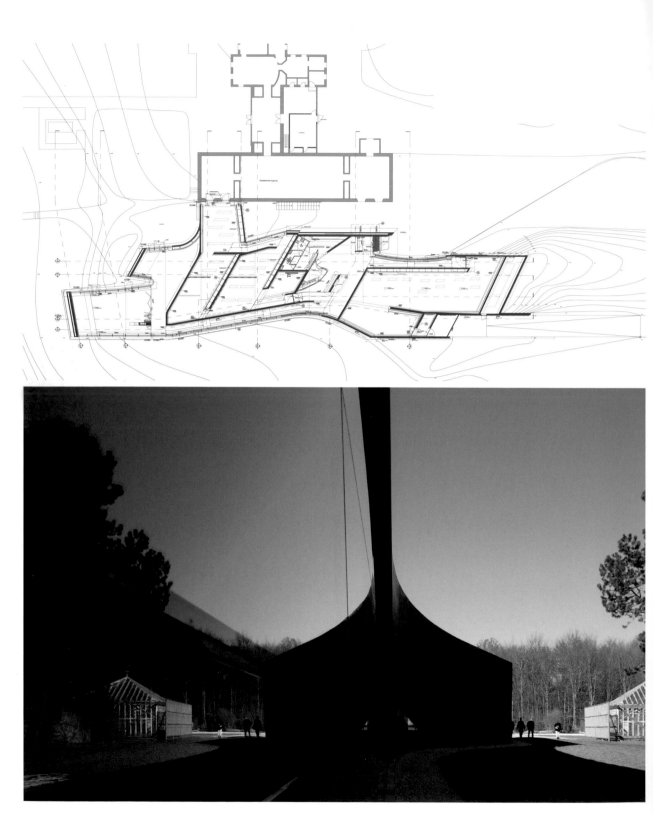

Hadid's architecture takes on forms that are far from the geometric rigidity of the original buildings.

Below:
The ceilings become walls and broad glazing allows views of the natural setting.

Opposite top:
A plan of the complex with Hadid's extension at the bottom.

Opposite bottom:
The dramatic forms of the structure extend into the landscape.

2000–2005 ▸ **Phaeno Science Center**

Wolfsburg, Germany

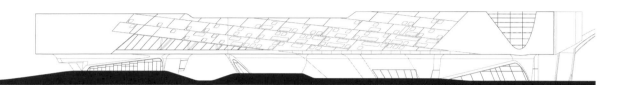

An elevation drawing shows the angled
supports and irregular openings of the
concrete volume.

Opposite page:
The angled, irregular form of the complex
gives it an almost organic appearance.

Below:
With its forward-leaning volume, the Phaeno
Center might bring to mind a great ship.

The client for this building was the City of Wolfsburg and the user, the Phaeno Founda-
tion. The construction cost was 79 million euros. Winner of an international competition in January 2000, Zaha Hadid imagined a structure that contains no less than
27000 cubic meters of concrete, and yet is suspended, in good part, some seven
meters above the ground. Explaining the unusual public space created beneath the Science Center, Hadid states: "The free ground is a modernist idea, but it was never an
animated space. That's what I try to create." Located near the town's central train station and across the tracks from the VW manufacturing plant, the new building rests on
10 asymmetrical cones, which contain a shop, a bar, and a bistro, as well as the museum entrance. The same cones penetrate the building and hold up the roof. The structure is nothing if not complex. Hadid states: "Phaeno is the most ambitious and complete statement of our quest for complex, dynamic, and fluid spaces. The visitor is
faced with a degree of complexity and strangeness, ruled by a very specific system
based on an unusual volumetric structural logic." As it is described by the users:
"Phaeno provides hands-on, entertaining access to the phenomena of natural science
and the principles of technology. Around 180000 visitors are expected to play and
experiment each year with its over 300 exhibits in the visitor labs, in the Ideas Forum,
and in the Science Theater." Total visitor space is 9000 square meters with 5900
square meters devoted to the "exhibition landscape"; 54 square meters and 10 workplaces for the biology and chemistry lab; 118 square meters and 16 workplaces for the
physics and technology lab; a 560-square-meter, 250-seat Science Theater; and the
370-square-meter Ideas Forum. Obviously sensitive to questions raised about the
complexity of the building, Hadid declares: "Nobody thinks that landscape is strange
because God made it, but if I make it, people think it's strange."

Supported by the large oblique columns, a vast
interior space allows for varied exhibitions.

Below:
The apparent irregularity of the structure is, in
fact, highly organized and functional.

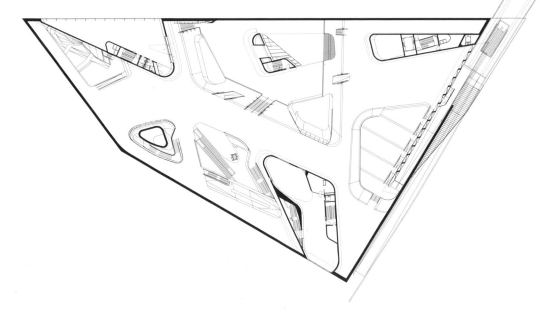

The forward-leaning aspect of the overall building is reflected in the interiors.

Below:
With its unexpected openings, the building takes on an appearance like that of a spacecraft.

2001–2005 ▸ **BMW Central Building**

Leipzig, Germany

The entry building reflects a continuous process of movement.

Above right:
A first-floor plan level +5.50 meters.

Opposite top:
The roof covering envelops the building, becoming its walls.

Opposite bottom:
With slanted columns, the whole structure appears to be moving forward.

Simply put, in the words of the architect: "It was the client's objective to translate industrial architecture into an aesthetic concept that complies equally with representational and functional requirements. In the transition zones between manufacturing halls and public space the Central Building acts as a 'mediator,' impressing a positive permanent impact upon the eye of the beholder in a restrained semiotic way." Zaha Hadid was asked to design this building, described as the "nerve center of the whole factory complex," subsequent to an April 2002 competition she won, when the layout of adjacent manufacturing buildings had already been decided. Suppliers chosen for the rest of the factory provided many prefabricated elements, in harmony with the "industrial approach to office spaces" decided by BMW. Used as the entrance to the entire plant, the Central Building connects the three main manufacturing departments. The nerve center concept is rendered all the more clear in that "the central area as a 'marketplace' is intended to enhance communication by providing staff with an area in which to avail themselves of personal and administrative services." A system of cascading floors allows views of different parts of the manufacturing process, ranging from assembly to the auditing area, described as "a central focus of everybody's attention." The building itself is made with "self-compacting concrete and a roof structure assembled with a series of H-steel beams." The architect intends to use the architecture to create an "overall transparency of the internal organization," but also to mix functions "to avoid the traditional segregation of status groups." Particular attention was also paid to the inevitable parking area in front of the building by "turning it into a dynamic spectacle in its own right."

2001–2006 ▸ **Maggie's Centre Fife**

Kirkcaldy, Fife, Scottland, UK

Irregular, triangular openings allow light into the building from above and from the sides.

Opposite page:
Maggie's Centre is intended as a "gateway to the surrounding landscape."

Maggie's Centres are a network of cancer care facilities in the United Kingdom founded by and named after Maggie Keswick Jencks, the late wife of the architecture critic Charles Jencks. An emphasis on architectural quality has been placed on recent designs, including Frank O. Gehry's first building in the United Kingdom, the Maggie's Centre in Dundee, and the new building in London, at Charing Cross Hospital, by Richard Rogers. Maggie's Centre Fife was the first building by Zaha Hadid to be built in the United Kingdom. Located at Victoria Hospital in Kirkcaldy, the brief required a "relaxed atmosphere where people can access additional support outside of the more clinical hospital environment." Hadid knew Maggie Keswick Jencks and says: "She had a unique ability to make everyone feel special by giving them the time and space to express and be themselves. As a friend of mine, it was important that this unique quality was in some way translated into my design for Maggie's Fife. I hope that the look and feel of the center in some way enhances a visitor's experience and provides a warm and welcoming place for them to relax and access the support they need." Located at the edge of a hollow area, the building is envisaged as a transitional space between the natural environment and the neighboring hospital. Hadid used a folding surface to link the two different environments, and shimmering black ceiling and walls, coated with black liquid polyurethane with silicon carbide grit combined with translucent and clear glass elevations. Sharply angled overhangs and a concrete plinth that extends into the site emphasize the feeling of continuity created by the architect.

Below right:
The folded shapes of the building with its triangular openings.

Below:
Image of a model of the center.

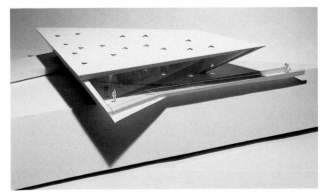

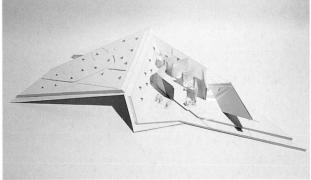

Innsbruck, Austria

Opposite page:
The shapes of the architecture are inspired by natural ice formations.

Below:
The Alpenzoo Station seen from below. A series of renders showing the relationship between the flowing forms.

Inaugurated on December 1, 2007, the Nordpark Cable Railway consists of four new stations and a cable-stayed suspension bridge over the River Inn. The roof surface of the four stations built for the INKB (Innsbrucker Nordkettenbahnen GmbH) Public Private Partnership is a total of 2500 square meters. The railway runs from the Congress Station in the center of the city, up the Nordkette Mountain to the Hungerburg Station, 288 meters above Innsbruck. Hadid had previously completed the Bergisel Ski Jump in the Austrian city (1999–2002; page 38). The architect won a 2005 competition for the Nordpark project together with the contractor Strabag. Adapting her designs to the specific locations of each station, Zaha Hadid employed "an overall language of fluidity." According to the architect: "We studied natural phenomena, such as glacial moraines and ice movements, as we wanted each station to use the fluid language of natural ice formations, like a frozen stream on the mountainside." Double-curvature glass on top of concrete plinths forms an "artificial landscape." Recently available fabrication methods, such as CNC milling and glass thermoforming, allowed the use of computer design and production with some techniques borrowed from the automotive industry.

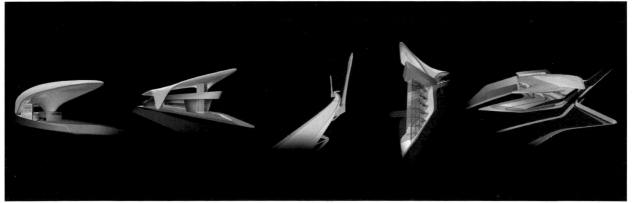

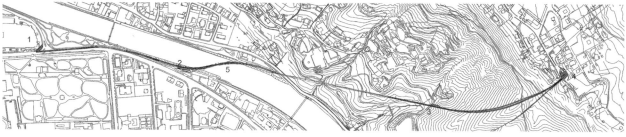

Above top:
A night view of the Hungerburg Station.

Above below:
Plan: stations # 1–5
1. Congress
2. Löwenhaus
3. Alpenzoo
4. Hungerburg
5. Innbrücke

Left:
Below its freely formed canopy, the Hungerburg Station.

A night view of the Löwenhaus Station.

The Löwenhaus Station with its associated bridge.

2007–2011 ▸ Mobile Art – Chanel Contemporary Art Container

Hong Kong, China; Tokyo, Japan; New York, New York, USA; Paris, France

As always with Hadid's work, there is an intimate relation between exterior and interior.

Opposite page:
The pavilion seen in its Central Park setting, New York.

Right:
A drawing shows the oyster-like layers of the structure.

Commissioned by Chanel designer Karl Lagerfeld, this traveling exhibition pavilion "is a celebration of the iconic work of Chanel, unmistakable for its smooth layering of exquisite details that together create an elegant, cohesive whole." Made of a series of continuous arch-shaped elements with a 65-square-meter central courtyard and a partially glazed adjustable ceiling, the pavilion is described as a "new artificial landscape for art installations." Twenty-nine meters long with a usable floor area of 700 square meters, the structure is six meters high, with a floor raised one meter above ground level. Conceived for easy dismounting and shipment, the Chanel pavilion has structural segments with a maximum width of 2.25 meters. Inspired to some extent by Chanel's famous quilted 2.55 handbag, the pavilion was erected in Hong Kong in March 2008, when Hadid commented: "The complexity and technological advances in digital imaging software and construction techniques have made the architecture of the Mobile Art pavilion possible. It is an architectural language of fluidity and nature, driven by new digital design, and manufacturing processes have enabled us to create the pavilion's totally organic forms—instead of the serial order of repetition that marks the architecture of the industrial 20th century." In 2007, Karl Lagerfeld said of Hadid: "She is the first architect to find a way to part with the all-dominating post-Bauhaus aesthetic. The value of her designs is similar to that of great poetry. The potential of her imagination is enormous." In 2010, the Pavilion was donated to the Institut du Monde Arabe in Paris as a permanent structure called Mobile Art.

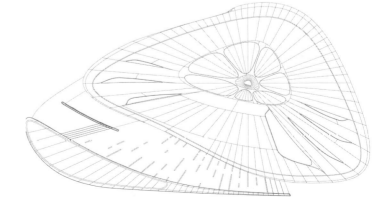

2005–2008 ▸ Zaragoza Bridge Pavilion

Zaragoza, Spain

The Zaragoza structure is the only inhabited bridge in Spain.

Opposite page:
The superimposed cladding panels are inspired by shark skin.

Right:
The actual pedestrian bridge has a surface area of 2500 square meters.

This interactive exhibition structure with a focus on water and sustainability, the themes of Expo 2008 in Zaragoza, has a total floor area of 6415 square meters, and an exhibition area of 3915 square meters. The pedestrian bridge that is part of the scheme occupies a further 2500 square meters. The pavilion is "organized around four main objects or pods that perform both as structural elements and as spatial enclosures." Each diamond-shaped pod corresponds to a specific exhibition area. Because loads are distributed between the pods rather than being borne by a central element, the resulting load-bearing members can be smaller. The bridge section of the pavilion spans 85 meters, from an Ebro River island to the Expo site. The architect explains: "The long pod that houses the pedestrian bridge spans 185 meters from the right riverbank to the bridge's middle support on an island, where the three exhibition pods are grafted on, spanning from the island to the left bank." Interiors vary from softly lit, air-conditioned enclosures focused on the works exhibited, to open, naturally ventilated areas with views of the river and the exhibition grounds. Twenty-six thousand flat panels organized in 300 different color combinations cover the upper part of the bridge, forming an array of optical patterns reminiscent of the skin of a shark. The lower part of the structure is constituted by a 275-meter long double-curved structural monocoque steel deck. While a number of Hadid's buildings have had a deep relation to the land, this form appears to move across the river in an almost organic flow, taking in the air and water that surrounds it.

Above:
The visible support elements of the bridge seem to blend mechanical and organic elements.

Left:
Smooth, sweeping surfaces alternate with complex openings that show the structure.

A worker on the roof of the bridge shows its large scale.

Below:
The two main sections respectively span 155 and 125 meters.

1998–2010 ▸ MAXXI: National Museum of XXI Century Arts

Rome, Italy

The client for this project is the Italian Ministry of Culture. Given the date of its conception, its forms may be more related to earlier work of Zaha Hadid, such as her Landscape Formation One (LF One, 1996–99; page 32), than to her most recent designs. The difference here is, of course, the location is no longer related to a natural setting, but rather to the city. Hadid's description of the project explains: "By intertwining the circulation with the urban context, the building shares a public dimension with the city, overlapping tendril-like paths and open space. In addition to the circulatory relationship, the architectural elements are also geometrically aligned with the urban grids that join at the site." Allowing both visitors and curators a good deal of freedom for their movement through the space, or interpretation of its potential, Hadid further explains: "The drift through the center is a trajectory through varied ambiences, filtered spectacles, and differentiated luminosity. Whilst offering a new freedom in the curators' palette, this in turn digests and recomposes the experience of art spectatorship as liberated dialogue with artifact and environment." The idea of drifting through the space is essential to the concept of the building, as opposed to a predetermined set of "key points." Nor is this interpretation related only to the question of architecture. "We take

The lobby, running through the building like a canyon, as seen in this image.

Opposite page:
The main lobby from which all spaces are accessible.

Right:
The overlapping and intersecting lines of the project seen in a model photo.

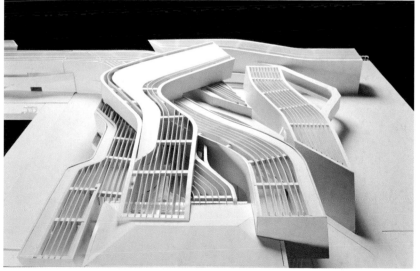

this opportunity, in the adventure of designing such a forward-looking institution, to confront the material and conceptual dissonance evoked by art practice since the late 1960s. The paths lead away from the 'object' and its correlative sanctifying, toward fields of multiple associations that are anticipative of the necessity to change," again according to the architect. The dissolution of such typical museum elements as the vertical wall intended to hang paintings here allows for walls that turn into ceilings or are transformed into windows. Surely related to the later work that provides for flowing spatial continuity, the MAXXI might be considered a transition toward that increasingly marked theme in Zaha Hadid's work.

An open square opposite the main entrance.

Lifting up on light pilotis, the building makes way for pedestrians and visitors.

The MAXXI is intended to "reinterpret existing urban grids."

Below:
Both in the drawing below and the image to its right, the concept of free flowing forms is apparent.

2009 ▸ **Burnham Pavilion**

Chicago, Illinois, USA

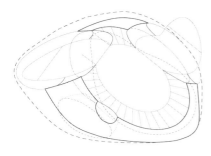

A plan drawing reveals the formal intricacy of the design.

Opposite page:
The shell-like structure appears in contrast to the nearby orthogonal towers of Chicago.

Below:
The 120-square-meter pavilion takes on a wide variety of colors at night.

One of a number of small structures commissioned to celebrate the 100th anniversary of the Burnham Plan for Chicago, this pavilion is made of bent aluminum. Each element was shaped and welded while inner and outer fabric skins were wrapped around this skeleton. The architect suggests that the structure contains "hidden traces of Burnham's organizational structure." The fabric serves as a screen for video installations within the pavilion. Intended to be easily dismantled or recycled, the pavilion is also meant to be assembled in another location in the future. Zaha Hadid Architects states: "The presence of the new structure triggers the visitor's intellectual curiosity whilst an intensification of public life around and within the pavilion supports the idea of public discourse."

1997–2010 ▸ **Sheikh Zayed Bridge**

Abu Dhabi, UAE

The arches of the bridge seem to rise above its deck and then plunge below the waters.

Above:
A sketch of the project by Zaha Hadid.

Opposite page:
Night lighting allows the bridge to gradually change hues.

This bridge, intended to link Abu Dhabi Island with the mainland, including Dubai and the international airport, has presented an engineering challenge with its sculptural forms, the complex geometry of its steel arches, and solid concrete piers. As Hadid's office description has it: "A collection, or strands of structures, gathered on one shore, are lifted and 'propelled' over the length of the channel. A sinusoidal waveform provides the structural silhouette shape across the channel." The main 234-meter-long arch of the bridge rises to a height of 60 meters above the water with the road some 40 meters below that. The four-lane structure with pedestrian walkways in each direction is the third bridge to link Abu Dhabi Island to the mainland, and is 68 meters in width, and a total of 842 meters long. Although other architects like Ben van Berkel have designed major bridges (UNStudio, Erasmus Bridge, Rotterdam, The Netherlands, 1996), Hadid's foray into this area, often reserved for engineers, is a confirmation of the range of her interests and ability to renew particularly codified structural forms. Where bridges often have static, symmetrical forms for reasons of stability, Hadid dares here to introduce complex notions of movement into the design. The project description makes this dynamic element apparent: "The mainland is the launch pad for the bridge structure emerging from the ground and approach road. The road decks are cantilevered on each side of the spine structure. Steel arches rise and spring from mass concrete piers asymmetrically, in length, between the road decks to mark the mainland and the navigation channels. The spine splits and splays from one shore along the central void position, diverging under the road decks to the outside of the roadways at the other end of the bridge."

2006–2010 ▸ **Evelyn Grace Academy**

London, UK

The Evelyn Grace Academy is a 10 745-square-meter facility that groups together four schools and is located in the Brixton area in a mainly residential district bordering two large roads. Funded by the Department for Education, the Academy is owned and operated by the registered charity Absolute Return for Kids (ARK). ARK was created by the French financier Arpad Busson and prides itself on rigid discipline and academic rigor. Natural light and ventilation is privileged in the new building, which opened in September 2010, as are "durable textures." The four schools share communal spaces encouraging "social communication with aggregation nodes that weave together the extensive accommodation schedule." There are also informal social and teaching areas that are meant to bring these two aspects of school life into closer contact. Sports facilities are also in close contact with the building, visible from the interior, stimulating interest in the physical as well as intellectual formation of students. Sweeping glazed surfaces and angled supports and façade elements give the complex a touch that is typical of the work of Zaha Hadid—a forward leaning dynamic image that surely contributes to stimulating the young people who study there. The building was the winner of the 2011 Royal Institute of British Architects Stirling Prize.

Open spaces and bright colors animate the interiors.

Opposite page:
A training track appears to go right through the school.

Right:
An overall plan of the facility.

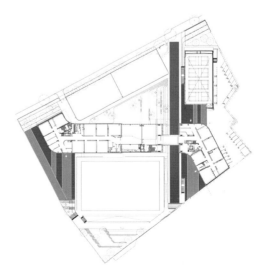

2003–2010 ▸ Guangzhou Opera House

Guangzhou, China

Located near the Tourist Park Island and Zhujiang Boulevard, the Opera House stands out.

Opposite page:
An internal street cuts through the complex linking to a future museum site.

Built for the Guangzhou Municipal Government, this is a 70 000-square-meter structure overlooking the Pearl River in the Guangzhou cultural development area. Guangzhou (also known in English as Canton), a city of nearly 10 million people and a river port, is located 120 kilometers northwest of Hong Kong. The site of the opera house, adjacent to a proposed municipal museum and a "metropolitan activities zone," is set against the background of the tall buildings of Zhujiang New Town, a particularly spectacular location leading to the Haixinsha Tourist Park Island. The architect speaks of a "twin boulder design" and of landforms to describe the facility that includes a 1800-seat grand theater, entrance lobby, lounge, multifunction hall, and support facilities. An internal street leading on one side to the future museum site has a café, bar, restaurant, and retail areas on one side, dividing the two main volumes. Inscribed in the urban context of the changing city in a strategic location at the foot of Zhujiang Boulevard, a central avenue of the city, the architectural design also adapts a variation on Hadid's theme of forms inspired by the land. Currently the largest performing arts center in South China and one of the three biggest theaters in the country, the Guangzhou Opera House is Zaha Hadid's first completed work in China.

Above:
A light, spatially spectacular foyer area in the 70 000-square-meter building.

Below:
A dance rehearsal space in use.

Opposite top:
The interior of the main auditorium.

Opposite bottom:
A section drawing shows the main concert hall to the right.

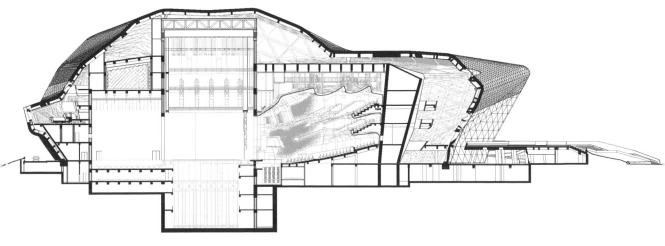

2005–2011 ▸ **CMA CGM Tower**

Marseille, France

Opposite page:
The 94 000-square-meter building stands out from its harbor setting.

Below:
A section drawing of the entire complex.

Below right:
The building is located on a site surrounded by heavily traveled roads.

CMA CGM is the world's third-largest container shipping company. Zaha Hadid was selected as designer of the new CMA CGM headquarters building in Marseille in November 2004. Describing a sweeping arc rising up from the ground to a height of 100 meters, the tower has a double façade system, a "fixed structural core," and a "peripheral array of columns that results in a dynamic symbiosis." The architect describes the project as a "vertical icon" intended to interact with old landmarks of the city, such as the Basilica of Notre-Dame-de-la-Garde and the Château d'If. A considerable amount of attention is paid in the description to the connectivity of the tower with pedestrian, water, and vehicular access to the site, emphasizing its interaction with the city. The form of the tower allows for larger floor plates in its lower areas while "the curving profiles act together with the core to provide a rigid frame and give a sense of movement and freedom to a new typology of tower." Marseille, like most other French cities, has shown little of the enthusiasm of other European centers for tall buildings but the CMA CGM building stands out in the city skyline, creating the sort of corporate visibility that most clients dream of. Nor is Marseille really a city known for its contemporary architecture, an image likely to change thanks to this tower.

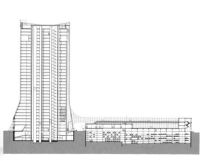

2004–2011 ▸ **Glasgow Riverside Museum**

Glasgow, Scotland, UK

The site drawing above appears inverted as opposed to the photo on its right.

Top right:
The wave or pleat motion of the plan is evident in this aerial photo.

Opposite top:
The ends of the building are fully glazed, in contrast to the undulating shell.

Opposite bottom:
Despite its sophistication, the museum also refers to harbor architecture.

Built for the Glasgow City Council at 22 Trongate in Glasgow, this 11 000-square-meter museum has 7000 square meters of exhibition space. The architect speaks of a "wave" or a "pleated movement" in describing the building that has a café and corporate entertainment space at one end with a view of the River Clyde. As it is described: "The building, open at opposite ends, positions itself in a tunnel-like configuration between the city and the Clyde. In doing so it becomes porous to its context. However, the connection from one to the other is where the building diverts to create a journey away from the external context into the world of the exhibits. Here the interior path becomes a mediator between the city and the river that can either be hermetic or porous depending on the exhibition layout. Thus the museum positions itself symbolically and functionally as open and fluid with its engagement of context and content." The office has also proposed a landscape scheme for the area around the building that develops the idea of a single surface laid across the site, with fluid changes in levels and blurred boundaries between hard and soft landscape. A shallow pond to the west side, to be used occasionally by boat enthusiasts, further links the building with the Clyde and the museum's visitors. One of a number of projects by recognized architects in Glasgow, the Museum of Transport Riverside Project underlines the desire of the city to confirm and develop its position as the cultural capital of Scotland.

An exhibition of bicycles takes on the mood of the soaring spaces created by Zaha Hadid.

Left:
Cars and tramways are placed in close proximity.

The display takes into account the pleats in the structure and participates in the forward movement of the architecture.

Right:
Displays are conceived in harmony with the sweeping lines of the interior of the building.

2005–2011 ▸ **London Aquatics Centre**

London, UK

Opposite top:
The sweeping aluminum roof covering of the complex forms walls as it descends to the ground.

Opposite bottom:
The building has an undeniably "aquatic" form even if no specific reference to water emerges.

Below:
A plan of the complex showing the 50-meter swimming pool and 25-meter diving pool.

This facility for the Aquatics Centre for the 2012 Olympic Games and future use has an area of 24 000 square meters. Zaha Hadid makes it clear that the architecture in this instance is "inspired by the fluid geometry of water in motion." An undulating roof rises from the ground and encloses the swimming pools in a "unifying gesture of fluidity." Part of the Olympic Park master plan, the facility is located on its southeastern corner. Pedestrian bridges crossing a canal will connect the London Aquatics Centre to the rest of the park. The structure is laid out perpendicular to the Stratford City Bridge and contains three pools, one for training, one for the swimming events, and the other for diving—with seating for 17 500 people for the main competition pool and diving, and 5000 seats for water polo. Other planned elements are contained in a podium. The steel and aluminum roof with double-curvature parabolic arches is most probably the "signature" element of the complex, filled with glazing where it rises above the podium. The interior of the roof is to be clad in timber. Hadid's participation in the Olympic program is a clear indication that she has taken on a significant position in architecture in the United Kingdom. Despite the complexity of the roof design, construction of the building began in July 2008 and was completed in July 2011.

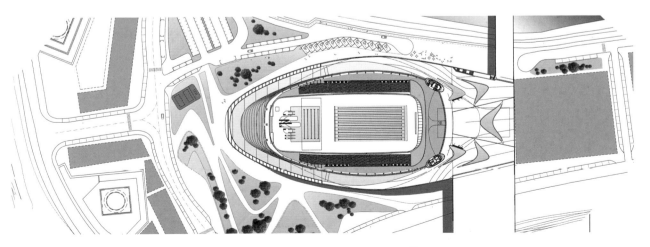

Left:
Even the diving boards have the distinctive touch of Zaha Hadid.

Below:
The main 50-meter swimming pool with the diving area in the background to the left.

Right:
The second 50-meter pool in the complex.

Below:
Angled glazing opens to the main swimming
pool and diving area.

2009–2011 ▸ Roca London Gallery

London, UK

MAIN ENTRANCE

The east elevation of the exterior of the Roca London Gallery.

Opposite page:
Cutting-edge lighting, audiovisual, and sound equipment is used in the gallery.

Below left:
A desk designed by the architect fits into the flowing interior volume.

Below right:
The architect refers to "three almost organic portals" to describe the façade of the gallery.

The 1100-square-meter Roca London Gallery is located at Station Court, Imperial Wharf, near Chelsea Harbour. Roca is a leading international bathroom products company and manufacturer of ceramic wall and floor tiles. In the past they have called on such designers as Rafael Moneo, David Chipperfield, and Herzog & de Meuron. Given the location of the single-level gallery and the business of the client, Zaha Hadid logically made water in all its forms the theme of this design. "Our work imbues architecture with the intricacy and beauty of natural forms," she states. "Using a formal language derived from the movement of water, the Roca London Gallery has been eroded and polished by fluidity, generating a sequence of dynamic spaces carved from this fascinating interplay between architecture and nature." The gray façade of the gallery with its three openings announces the theme of erosion. The freely flowing central space is clad in all-white faceted GRP (gypsum) panels. More intimate, connected spaces can be viewed from this main display area. The facility is intended to be more than a static exhibition gallery for Roca. Meetings, presentations, seminars, and debates are among the planned activities. Zaha Hadid has fully adapted her work to the needs and profession of the client in a convincing way.

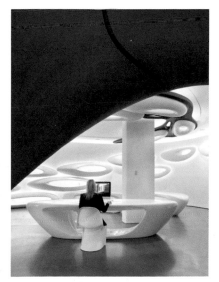

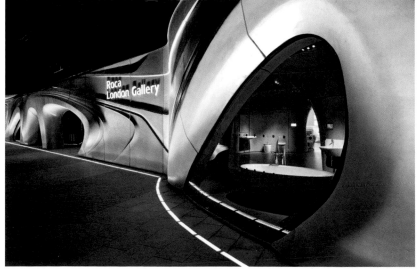

Life and Work

Zaha Hadid studied architecture at the Architectural Association (AA) in London beginning in 1972 and was awarded the Diploma Prize in 1977. She became a partner of the Office for Metropolitan Architecture, taught at the AA with OMA collaborators Rem Koolhaas and Elia Zenghelis, and later led her own studio at the AA until 1987. Since then she has held the Kenzo Tange Chair at the Graduate School of Design, Harvard University; the Sullivan Chair at the University of Illinois, School of Architecture, Chicago; guest professorships at the Hochschule für Bildende Künste in Hamburg; the Knolton School of Architecture, Ohio; and the Masters Studio at Columbia University, New York. In addition, she was made Honorary Member of the American Academy of Arts and Letters, Fellow of the American Institute of Architecture, and Commander of the British Empire, 2002. She is currently Professor at the University of Applied Arts in Vienna, Austria, and was the Eero Saarinen Visiting Professor of Architectural Design at Yale University, New Haven, Connecticut.

In 2004, Zaha Hadid became the first woman to win the coveted Pritzker Prize. Well known for her paintings and drawings, she had substantial influence even before beginning to build prodigiously.

In 2011, Hadid completed the London Aquatics Centre for the 2012 Olympic Games and the CMA CGM Headquarters tower in Marseille, France. Current projects she is working on include the High-Speed Train Stations in Naples and Durango; the Fiera di Milano master plan and tower as well as master-planning projects in Beijing, Bilbao, Istanbul, and Singapore. In the Middle East, Hadid's portfolio includes national cultural and research centers in Jordan, Morocco, Algeria, Azerbaijan, Abu Dhabi, and Saudi Arabia, as well as the new Central Bank of Iraq.

Bibliography

Hadid's work is widely published in periodicals and monographs, which include:

"Zaha Hadid," *GA Architect (no. 5, 1986, Japan)*
Zaha Hadid: Planetary Architecture II, *AA files (no. 6, 1984)*
"Zaha Hadid 1983–1991," *El Croquis (no. 52, 1991, Madrid)*
"Zaha M Hadid," *GA Document Extra, (no. 3, 1995, Japan)*
"Zaha Hadid 1992–1995," *El Croquis (no. 73, 1995, Madrid)*
"Zaha Hadid 1996–2001," *El Croquis (no. 103, 2001, Madrid)*
Zaha Hadid: The Complete Buildings and Projects (London, UK, 1998)
Zaha Hadid: LF One (Basel, Switzerland, 1999)
Architecture of Zaha Hadid in photographs by Helene Binet (Baden, Switzerland, 2000)
GA Document (nos. 65 and 66. Japan, 2001)
Zaha Hadid, Opere e Progetti (Turin, 2002)
Zaha Hadid Architektur (MAK, Vienna, Austria, 2003)
Zaha Hadid Space for Art (Baden, Switzerland, 2004)
"Zaha Hadid 1983–2004," *El Croquis (2004, Madrid)*
Digital Hadid. Landscapes in Motion (Basel, Switzerland, 2004)
Car Park and Terminus Strasbourg (Baden, Switzerland, 2004)
Zaha Hadid Complete Works (London, UK, 2004)
BMW Central Building (Princeton, USA, 2006)
Zaha Hadid, Catalog for the Solomon R. Guggenheim Museum (2006)
GA Document, Special Issue, Zaha Hadid (no. 99, 2007, Japan)
Zaha Hadid (Milan, Italy, 2007)
Total Fluidity, Catalog for Seoul Design Olympiad Exhibition (2008)
Zaha Hadid: Complete Works 1979–2009 (Cologne, 2009)

Zaha Hadid, 2008
Photograph by Gautier Deblonde

Zaha Hadid and Patrik Schumacher, 2009
Photograph by Morley von Sternberg

Collaborators

Moonsoon Restaurant
Design Team: Zaha Hadid with Bill Goodwin, Shin Egashira, Kar Hwa, Ho, Edgar González, Bryan Langlands, Ed Gaskin, Yuko Moriyama, Urit Luden, Craig Kiner, Dianne Hunter-Gorman, Patrik Schumacher

Vitra Fire Station
Design: Zaha Hadid; *Project Architect*: Patrik Schumacher; *Detail Design*: Patrik Schumacher, Signy Svalastoga; *Design Team*: Simon Koumjian, Edgar González, Kar Wha Ho, Voon Yee-Wong, Craig Kiner, Cristina Verissimo, Maria Rossi, Daniel R. Oakley, Nicola Cousins, David Gomersall, Olaf Weishaupt

Landscape Formation One
Design: Zaha Hadid with Patrik Schumacher; *Project Architect*: Markus Dochantschi; *Project Team*: Oliver Domeisen, Wassim Halabi, Garin O'Aivazian, Barbara Pfenningstorff, James Lim

Mind Zone Millennium Dome
Design: Zaha Hadid; *Project Architect*: Jim Heverin
Project Team: Barbara Kuit, Jon Richards, Paul Butler, Ana Sotrel, Christos Passas, Graham Modlen, Oliver Domeisen; *Artist Liaison*: Doris Lockhart-Saatchi

Hoenheim-Nord Terminus and Car Park
Design: Zaha Hadid; *Project Architect*: Stéphane Hof; *Sketch Design Team*: Stéphane Hof, Sara Klomps, Woody K.T. Yao, Sonia Villaseca; *Project Team*: Silvia Forlati, Patrik Schumacher, Markus Dochantschi, David Salazar, Caroline Voet, Eddie Can, Stanley Lau, David Gerber, Chris Dopheide, Edgar Gonzáles

Bergisel Ski Jump
Design: Zaha Hadid; *Project Director*: Markus Dochantschi; *Project Architect*: Jan Hübener; *Project Team*: Matthias Frei, Cedric Libert, Silvia Forlati, Jim Heverin, Garin O'Aivazian, Sara Noel Costa de Araujo

Lois & Richard Rosenthal Center for Contemporary Art
Design: Zaha Hadid; *Project Architect*: Markus Dochantschi; *Assistant Project Architect*: Ed Gaskin; *Project Team*: Ana Sotrel, Jan Hübener, David Gerber, Christos Passas, Sonia Villaseca, James Lim, Jee-Eun Lee, Oliver Domeisen, Helmut Kinzler, Patrik Schumacher, Michael Wolfson, David Gomersall

Ordrupgaard Museum Extension
Design: Zaha Hadid; *Project Architect*: Ken Bostock; *Design Team*: Caroline Krogh Andersen

Phaeno Science Centre
Design: Zaha Hadid with Christos Passas; *Project Architect*: Christos Passas; *Assistant Project Architect*: Sara Klomps; *Special Contributor*: Patrik Schumacher;

Project Team: Helmut Kinzler, Gernot Finselbach, David Salazar, Enrico Kleinke, Lida Charsouli, Barbara Kuit, Günter Barczik, Silvia Forlati, Ken Bostock, Liam Young, Edgar Gonzales, Markus Dochantschi

BMW Central Building
Design: Zaha Hadid with Patrik Schumacher; *Project Architects*: Jim Heverin, Lars Teichmann; *Project Team*: Matthias Frei, Jan Hübener, Annette Bresinsky, Manuela Gatto, Fabian Hecker, Cornelius Schlotthauer, Wolfgang Sunder, Anneka Wegener, Markus Planteu, Robert Neumayr, Christina Beaumont, Achim Gergen

Maggie's Centre Five
Design: Zaha Hadid; *Project Architects*: Jim Heverin, Tiago Correia

Nordpark Railway Stations
Design: Zaha Hadid with Patrik Schumacher; *Project Architect*: Thomas Vietzke; *Design Team*: Jens Borstelmann, Markus Planteu; *Production Team*: Caroline Andersen, Makakrai Suthadarat, Marcela Spadaro, Anneka Wagener, Adriano De Gioannis, Peter Pichler, Susann Berggren

Mobile Art – Chanel Contemporary Art Container
Design: Zaha Hadid with Patrik Schumacher; *Project Architects*: Thomas Vietzke, Jens Borstelmann; *Project Team*: Helen Lee, Claudia Wulf, Erhan Patat, Tetsuya Yamasaki, Daniel Fiser

Zaragoza Bridge Pavilion
Design: Zaha Hadid with Patrik Schumacher; *Project Architect*: Manuela Gatto; *Project Team*: Fabian Hecker, Matthias Baer, Soohyun Chang, Ignacio Choliz, Federico Dunkelberg, Maria José Mendoza, José M. Monfa, Marta Rodriguez, Diego Rosales, Guillermo Ruiz, Lucio Santos, Hala Sheikh, Marcela Spadaro, Anat Stern, Jay Suthadarat

MAXXI: National Museum of XXI Century Arts
Design: Zaha Hadid with Patrik Schumacher; *Project Architect*: Gianluca Racana; *Project Team*: Anja Simons, Paolo Matteuzzi, Fabio Ceci, Mario Mattia, Maurizio Meossi, Paolo Zilli, Luca Peralta, Maria Velceva, Matteo Grimaldi, Ana M.Cajiao, Barbara Pfenningstorff, Dillon Lin, Ken Bostock, Raza Zahid, Lars Teichmann, Adriano De Gioannis, Amin Taha, Caroline Voet, Gianluca Ruggeri, Luca Segarelli

Burnham Pavilion
Design: Zaha Hadid with Patrik Schumacher; *Project Architect*: Jens Borstelmann, Thomas Vietzke; *Project Team*: Teoman Ayas, Evan Erlebacher

Sheikh Zayed Bridge
Design: Zaha Hadid; *Project Architect*: Graham

Modlen; *Project Team*: Garin O'Aivazian, Christos Passas, Patrik Schumacher, Sara Klomps, Zahira Nazer, Steve Power

Evelyn Grace Academy
Design: Zaha Hadid with Patrik Schumacher; *Project Director*: Lars Teichmann; *Project Architect*: Matthew Hardcastle; *Project Team*: Lars Teichmann, Matthew Hardcastle, Bidisha Sinha, Henning Hansen, Lisamarie Villegas, Ambia, Enrico Kleinke, Judith Wahle, Christine Chow, Guy Taylor, Patrick Bedarf, Sang Hilliges, Hoda Nobakhti

Guangzhou Opera House
Design: Zaha Hadid; *Project Directors*: Woody K.T. Yao, Patrik Schumacher; *Project Leader*: Simon Yu; *Project Team*: Jason Guo, Yang Jingwen, Long Jiang, Ta-Kang Hsu, Yi-Ching Liu, Zhi Wang, Christine Chow, Cyril Shing, Filippo Innocenti, Lourdes Sánchez, Hinki Kwong, Junkai Jian

CMA CGM Tower Marseille
Design: Zaha Hadid; *Project Director* Jim Heverin; *Project Architect*: Stephane Vallotton; *Project Team*: Karim Muallem, Simone Contasta, Leonie Heinrich, Alvin Triestanto, Muriel Boselli, Eugene Leung, Bhushan Mantri, Jerome Michel, Nerea Feliz, Prashanth Sridharan, Birgit Eistert, Evelyn Gono, Marian Ripoll

Glasgow Riverside Museum
Design: Zaha Hadid; *Project Director*: Jim Heverin; *Project Architect*: Johannes Hoffmann; *Project Team*: Matthias Frei, Agnes Koltay, Malca Mizrahi, Tyen Masten, Gemma Douglas, Daniel Baerlecken, Achim Gergen, Christina Beaumont, Markus Planteu, Claudia Wulf, Alasdair Graham, Rebecca Haines-Gadd, Brandon Buck, Naomi Fritz, Liat Muller, Elke Presser, Hinki Kwon, Michael Mader, Ming Cheong, Mikel Bennett, Jieun Lee, Chun Chiu, Aris Giorgiadis, Lole Mate, Thomas Hale, Andreas Helgesson, Andrew Summers, Des Fagan, Laymon Thaung

London Aquatics Centre
Design: Zaha Hadid; *Project Director*: Jim Heverin; *Project Architects*: Glenn Moorley, Sara Klomps; *Project Team*: Alex Bilton, Alex Marcoulides, Barbara Bochnak, Carlos Carijo, Clay Shorthall, Ertu Erbay, Giorgia Cannici, Hannes Schafelner, Hee Seung Lee, Kasia Townend, Nannette Jackowski, Nicholas Gdalewitch, Seth Handley, Thomas Soo, Tom Locke, Torsten Broeder, Tristan Job, Yamac Korfali, Yeena Yoon

Roca London Gallery
Design: Zaha Hadid with Patrik Schumacher; *Project Directors*: Woody Yao, Maha Kutay; *Project Architect*: Margarita Yordanova Valova

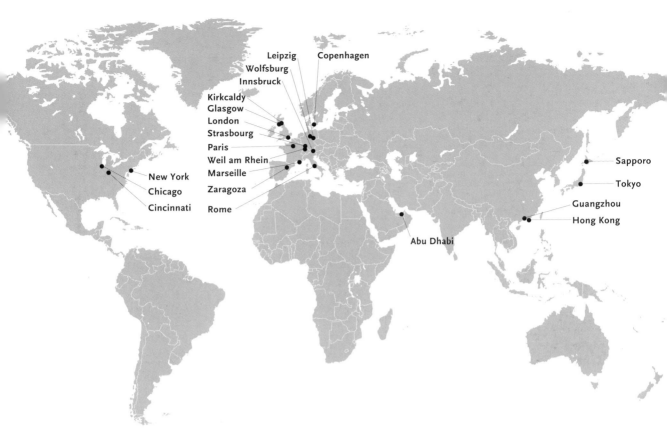

World Map

AUSTRIA
Innsbruck
▶ Bergisel Ski Jump
▶ Nordpark Railway Stations

CHINA
Guangzhou
▶ Guangzhou Opera House
Hong Kong
▶ Mobile Art – Chanel Contemporary
  Art Container

DENMARK
Copenhagen
▶ Ordrupgaard Museum Extension

FRANCE
Marseille
▶ CMA CGM Tower Marseille
Paris
▶ Mobile Art – Chanel Contemporary
  Art Container
Strasbourg
▶ Hoenheim-Nord Terminus and Car Park

GERMANY
Leipzig
▶ BMW Central Building
Weil am Rhein
▶ Vitra Fire Station
▶ Landscape Formation One (LF One)
Wolfsburg
▶ Phaeno Science Center

ITALY
Rome
▶ MAXXI: National Museum of
  XXI Century Arts

JAPAN
Sapporo
▶ Moonsoon Restaurant
Tokyo
▶ Mobile Art – Chanel Contemporary
  Art Container

SPAIN
Zaragoza
▶ Zaragoza Bridge Pavilion

UAE
Abu Dhabi
▶ Sheikh Zayed Bridge

UK
Glasgow
▶ Glasgow Riverside Museum
London
▶ Evelyn Grace Academy
▶ London Aquatics Centre
▶ Mind Zone Millennium Dome
▶ Roca London Gallery
Kirkcaldy, Fife
▶ Maggie's Centre Fife

USA
Chicago, Illinois
▶ Burnham Pavilion
Cincinnati, Ohio
▶ Lois & Richard Rosenthal Center
  for Contemporary Art
New York, New York
▶ Mobile Art – Chanel Contemporary
  Art Container

Prizes and Awards

1977	Graduated from the Architectural Association School of Architecture, London, AA Diploma Prize
1980	Founded Zaha Hadid Architects
1982	British Architecture Gold Medal for Architectural Design, for 59 Eaton Place
1998	Honorable Member of the Bund Deutscher Architekten
2000	Honorable Member of the American Academy of Arts and Letters
	Honorary Fellowship of the American Institute of Architects
	RIBA Award, for the project Mind Zone, Millennium Dome
2002	Equerre d'Argent, for Hoenheim-Nord Terminus
	Commander of the British Empire (CBE)
2003	Mies van der Rohe Award for European Architecture, for Hoenheim-Nord Terminus
2004	Laureate of the Pritzker Architecture Prize
2005	Honorary Fellow of Columbia University, New York
	Member of the Royal Academy of Arts, London
	Deutsche Architecture Prize, for the BMW Central Building
	Finalist RIBA Stirling Prize, for the BMW Central Building
	Gold Medal for Design, International Olympic Committee, for the Bergisel Ski Jump
	Austrian Decoration for Science and Art, Vienna
	Designer of the Year, Design 05 Miami
2006	Honorary Doctorate, Yale University, USA
	Honorary Doctorate, American University of Beirut
	RIBA Medal, European Cultural Building of the Year, for the Phaeno Science Center
	RIBA Jencks Award
	American Institute of Architects, UK Chapter Award, for the Phaeno Science Center
	Leading European Architects Forum, Best Structural Design, for the Phaeno Science Center

Finalist RIBA Stirling Prize, for the Phaeno Science Center
Academician, The International Academy of Architecture

2007	American Institute of Architects, UK Chapter Award, for Maggie's Centre Fife
	Finalist Mies van der Rohe Award for European Architecture, for the Phaeno Science Center
	Thomas Jefferson Foundation Medal in Architecture
	Scottish Design Award, Best Public Building, for Maggie's Centre Fife
	London Design Medal, Outstanding Contribution for Design
	Frame Magazine "Great Indoors" Award, for the Lopez de Heredia Winery
2008	Designer of the Year, Maison & Objet, Paris
	Dedalo Minosse International Prize, for the BMW Central Building
	Travel & Leisure Design Awards, Best Transport Building, for the project Nordpark Railway Stations
	Spirit of Achievement Award, New York
	Honorary Degree from the Pratt Institute, New York
	RIBA European Prize, for the Nordpark Railway Stations
	Cityscape Award, for the Signature Towers
	The Chicago Athenaeum, The International Architecture Award, for the project Maggie's Centre Fife
2009	Architectural Digest (Spain) Editor's Award
	Innovation & Design Awards, Conde Nast Traveller, for the Zaragoza Bridge Pavilion
	Laureate of the Praemium Imperiale
2010	Laureate of the RIBA Stirling Prize, for the MAXXI Museum in Rome
	Commander of the French Ordre des Arts et des lettres

Credits

Photographers and Illustrators:
Cover © Hufton + Crow; 14, 17, 19, 66, 67, 68 (below), 69, 77, 78, 81 © Iwan Baan; 2 © Jason Schmidt; 6, 18, 21, 22, 28, 30 (below), 31, 72, 73, 80 © Christian Richters; 7 © Simone Cecchetti; 8, 26, 27 © Paul Warchol; 9, 10, 30 (above), 32-36, 38, 42, 43, 52 (below), 53, 55 © Hélène Binet; 11, 76, 82 (below), 84 (below), 88, 89 © Hufton + Crow/VIEW; 12, 48-52, 54 (above), 56-59 © Werner Huthmacher; 13, 44-47 (above), 63, 64 (below), 65 © FS GUERRA; 15, 25, 39, 40, 62, 68 (above) © Roland Halbe; 20, 61, 79 © Virgile Simon Bertrand; 23, 82 (above), 84 (above), 85 © Alan McAteer; 24, 64 (above), 74, 75, 90, 91 © Luke Hayes; 37 © Airdiasol.Rothan; 47 (below) © Cristóbal Palma; 60 © John Linden; 70, 71 © Michelle Litvin; 83 © Hawkeye Aerial Photography; 92 © Gautier Deblonde; 93 © Morley von Sternberg; back cover © Henry Bourne

The Author

Philip Jodidio studied art history and economics at Harvard, and edited *Connaissance des Arts* for over 20 years. His books include TASCHEN's *Architecture Now!* series, and monographs on Tadao Ando, Norman Foster, Richard Meier, Jean Nouvel, and Zaha Hadid. He is internationally renowned as one of the most popular writers on the subject of architecture.